thebrewerybible.com | hello@thebrewerybible.com | @thebrewerybible

Published by Altum Media, 2019
altummedia.co.uk | hello@altummedia.co.uk | @altum.media

A catalogue record of this book is available from the British Library.

A special thanks is given to our amazing creative team;
- Editor and primary contributor, Adrian Tierney-Jones
- Book design, Judy Caley
- Cover design, Rosie Carmicheal
- Stirchley Beer Mile map, Emmy Lupin

To find out more about The Brewery Bible Ltd please visit thebrewerybible.com or follow us @thebrewerybible

Printed and bound by Short Run Press, Exeter on FSC-certified paper

978-1-9160828-1-6

THE BREWERY BIBLE

MIDLANDS EDITION 1

thebrewerybible.com

@thebrewerybible

The perfect gift for beer lovers
Explore the full range of books
Shop now at thebrewerybible.com
THE BREWERY BIBLE
SOUTH WEST EDITION I

Contents

7 Your beer adventure starts with us
9 From the Editor
10 Will walk for a beer
16 Purity Brewing
20 Celebrating Jaipur
24 A 33-mile beer adventure
30 Midlands Breweries Map
32 East Midlands
34 **#1 Black Iris Brewery**
36 **#2 Blue Monkey Brewery**
38 **#3 Buxton Brewery**
40 **#4 Charnwood Brewery**
42 **#5 Lincoln Green Brewing Company**
44 **#6 Peak Ales**
46 **#7 Langton Brewery**
48 **#8 Thornbridge Brewery**
50 #9 Brewhouse & Kitchen Sutton Coldfield
51 #10 Buxton Brewery Tap House & Cellar
52 #11 Hopology
53 #12 Six Barrel Drafthouse
54 #13 The Organ Grinder, Nottingham
55 #14 Thornbridge Taproom
56 East Midlands Breweries
60 **West Midlands**
62 **#15 Attic Brew Co.**
64 **#16 The Backyard Brewhouse**
66 **#17 Banks's Brewery**
68 **#18 Beat Brewery**
70 **#19 Birmingham Brewing Company**
72 **#20 Burning Soul**
74 **#21 Byatt's Brewery**
76 **#22 Dhillon's**
78 **#23 Enville Brewery**
80 **#24 Green Duck Beer Co.**
82 **#25 The Indian Brewery**
84 **#26 RAN Ales**
86 **#27 Sadler's Brewing Co.**
88 #28 Brewhouse & Kitchen Lichfield
89 #29 Brewhouse & Kitchen Nottingham
90 #30 KILDER
91 #31 Purecraft Bar & Kitchen
92 #32 The Wildcat Tap
94 West Midlands Breweries
96 Warwickshire & Northamptonshire
98 **#33 Great Oakley Brewery**
100 **#34 Maule Brewing Co.**
102 **#35 Purity Brewing Co**
104 **#36 Towcester Mill Brewery**
106 **#37 XT Brewing**
108 #38 beertorrent®
109 #39 The Drawing Board Bottle Shop
110 #40 The Drawing Board
112 Warwickshire & Northamptonshire Breweries
114 Staffordshire
116 **#41 Burton Bridge Brewery**
118 **#42 Burton Town Brewery**
120 **#43 Heritage Brewing**
122 **#44 Lymestone Brewery**
124 **#45 Marston's Brewery**
126 **#46 Slater's Ales**
128 #47 Candid Beer
129 #48 The Beer Hut
130 #49 The Bridge Inn
132 Staffordshire Breweries
134 Herefordshire, Worcestershire & Shropshire
136 **#50 Bewdley Brewery Ltd**
138 **#51 Joule's Brewery**
140 **#52 Ludlow Brewing Co.**
142 **#53 The Sociable Beer Company**
144 **#54 The Wood Brewery**
146 **#55 Wye Valley Brewery**
148 #56 Hop Lord's Tap room & Bottle Shop
149 #57 Red Lion Brewery Tap
150 #58 The Barrels
151 #59 The Firefly, Hereford
152 #60 The Firefly,Worcester
154 Herefordshire, Worcestershire & Shropshire Breweries
156 Meet the team
159 Tasting Notes

More on P28-29

Your beer adventure starts with us

The Brewery Bible exists to connect you directly to the best places and spaces serving the freshest local beer up and down the country. As the beer drinking experience continuously evolves, we will keep you in the know about the best brews, coolest tap rooms, in-depth tours and tastings happening in your local region and beyond.

Presented as a series of beautifully designed regional guides, a mobile-friendly website and a free-to-download app, The Brewery Bible is your ultimate companion when looking to discover, uncover and treasure the wonders of beer.

We will take you across the UK where you can explore over 2000 breweries, 700 brewery tap rooms, plus hand-picked venues and stockists pushing the boundaries and working with the leaders in beer to curate lip-smacking menus not to be missed.

With a growing emphasis on local provenance and craft, The Brewery Bible will help you wherever you are on your beer journey, from the curious to the converted. Sample the freshest beers in the country, right next to where they are made. You might even meet the brewer or tuck into a beer and food pairing to help you think about beer in a completely different way.

Gather some friends, open the map (page 30) or download our app and start planning your next beer adventure...

From the Editor

The first brewery that I ever visited was in the Midlands, the Highgate Brewery in Walsall, an old Victorian building that had been saved from closure. This was in 1997 and I recall being rather impressed by the grandness of the place. In the next couple of years, several other trips followed to the area, with visits to the Sarah Hughes Brewery and Holden's. I also visited various pubs, including the Waggon & Horses (how amazing it was then to see a pub with so many beers), and the lop-sided looking Crooked House between Dudley and Telford.

Since then I have kept in touch with beer and brewing trends in all parts of the Midlands, whether Nottingham and its thriving craft scene, Birmingham and its excellent pubs or regular forays to places such as Burton or Bakewell (where Thornbridge is based). You could say that I like drinking beer in the Midlands. It seems like it has a genuine pub culture that has become allied to the vibrancy of craft, which means you can get a strong dark mild, a blueberry IPA, good German or Czech-style lagers and brooding stouts and porters. The area is awash with great beers and breweries and The Brewery Bible is your essential guide to them.

Adrian Tierney-Jones

Will walk for a beer

The Stirchley Beer Mile, South Birmingham

The Romans liked the mile. It helped them work out distances when they were in a conquering mood. Beer-lovers also like the mile. There's the combination of running and drinking which is called the beer mile, but I don't think we need to concern ourselves about it here. Then there's the Beer Mile as in an approximate mile or so in somewhere like Bermondsey, where tap rooms, breweries, pubs and street food outlets are dotted about like so many milestones (which the Romans also liked). One of the latest Beer Miles to bring in those with a penchant for the perfect pint and an urge to drink in a space where the beer was made, is the Stirchley Beer Mile, which is a district in the South West part of Birmingham, close to Bournville.

At the moment there are eight venues, tap rooms for breweries, bottle shops and bars/pubs and they are open Friday evenings and Saturday afternoons/evenings. The route is easily covered if you get off at Bournville railway station (several stops from Birmingham New Street) and then head along Pershore Road and get a train back to Birmingham from Kings Norton station. It is growing in popularity and gives attendees a chance to catch a vibrant element of the Midlands craft beer scene. Here are its highlights as experienced by The Brewery Bible on a recent visit.

More information on the Beer Mile can be found at stirchleybeermile.wordpress.com (note that the website suggests starting at Kings Norton, but we started at the other end as it meant less distance to walk carrying beer from both the bottle shops).

1. Attic Brew Co.
29B Mary Vale Road B30 2DA
Large warehouse space on an industrial estate that was apparently a munitions factory in World War I. Inside, it's light and airy with the wooden bar and chalked beer list to one side and the brewing kit along the wall on the other side. Beers are 'classic styles with an English twist', so expect saisons, Weissbiers and Vienna lagers as well as IPAs.

2. The British Oak
1364 Pershore Road B30 2XS
Tradition calls for this classic Grade II listed pub which was remodelled in the 1920s, so expect oak wood panelling, leaded glass, snob screens and all the grandness of the great movement of 'pub improvement' after World War I. Cask beers and keg, including the likes of Timothy Taylor Landlord and Lagunitas IPA.

3. Cork & Cage
1373 Pershore Road B30 2JR
This is a one time barber's where a quick snip and would-you-like-something-for-the-weekend-sir has been swapped for a narrow, minimalist bar which specialises in lambic, sour and wild beer as well as modern beer styles from the likes of St Mars of the Desert and DEYA. Food is small plates of Turkish meze. Card only.

4. Wildcat Tap
1381-1383, Pershore Road B30 2JR
Once a restaurant but now a modern craft beer bar with five cask beers and seven keg, this spot mixes up stark minimalism with a warm cafeteria vibe. Beers come from the likes of Burning Soul, Burning Sky and Neptune, as well as many other stars of the craft beer scene. A place to concentrate on beer and good company and enjoy a friendly discussion on whether or not a milkshake IPA is better than a strong dark mild.

5. Birmingham Brewing Company
Unit 15, Stirchley Trading Estate,
Hazelwell Road, B30 2PF

Embed yourself in the confines of this award-winning brewery, which opens alternate weekends (check website for details), with the promise of beers such as Stout Brummie all of which are brewed on the premises. There is also a regular street food cart in attendance and children and dogs are welcome.

6. Stirchley Wines
1535-1537 Pershore Road, B30 2JH

Yes, wine is sold in this long-established drinks outlet but it's the beer choice that overwhelms with bottles and cans from around the UK, Europe, the USA and the rest of the world. Winner of many awards including Ratebeer and The Drinks Retaining Awards, Stirchley Wines was established in 1979 by Amrik Rajput and now run by son Krishan, who is a leading light in the Birmingham craft beer scene.

7. GlassHouse Beer
Unit 6b Waterside Business Park,
1649-1652, Pershore Road B30 3DR

Compact brewery and tap room with the brewing equipment at one end and a solid bar at the other. You can expect hop-forward beers including occasional collaborations with craft beer superstars including Cheltenham's DEYA.

8. Cotteridge Wines
1825 Pershore Road B30 3DN

Final stop on the mile before strolling down to Kings Norton is this excellent award-winning bottle shop which also has a tap room where up to a dozen beers can be sampled, an especially beneficent thing to do if the sun is shining and you can go into the small garden at the back. Both this and Stirchley Wines are close to the final station and offer a great take-home example of the beer choice on the Mile.

Birmingham Brewing Company
5
2
The British Oak
3
Cork and Cage
4
Wildcat Tap
Stirchley Wines & Spirits
6
1
Attic Brew Co.
Bournville Station
Birmingham

Stirchley Beer Mile

Purity Brewing

Where sustainability meets community

Sustainability is a crucial part of a brewery's make-up these days. Brewing itself uses up a lot of energy and the best practice target within the British brewing industry is three pints to make one. Consumers are also keen to see that their favourite brewers are doing their bit for the environment.

One of the most ecologically aware breweries in the Midlands (or even the UK) is Purity Brewing, who on their foundation in 2005 were absolutely clear over the way they wanted to go.

'Myself and co-brewery founder Jim are passionate about sustainability and always have been,' says Purity CEO Paul Halsey. 'We could have set up a brewery in an industrial estate and had a bigger and more sensible set-up for a business with the ability to grow easier, but could we have been sustainable and have a wetland system like we have? No.

'This was all about regeneration and sustainability and it permeates throughout our business from the spent grain, hops and yeast all recycled within the local farming community (including our own), through to our wetland system which takes our used water, cleans it through a series of pools, before ending back in the River Arrow as pure water.

'We continue to review the materials we use and reduce our use of plastics. We're currently trialing a cardboard can topper, to remove the use of plastic. We're always looking to reduce our water consumption and our BrauKon brew-kit helps us to do that.'

Looking around the industry, more breweries are becoming aware of their brewing processes and how they impact on the environment. Last year Carlsberg dispensed with the plastic rings for multi-can packs, replacing them with a special glue that holds the cans together. Lower down the brewing ladder, many smaller breweries have long sent out used grains and hops to farmers and gardeners. This is all something that Halsey is happy to encourage.

Purity

'We would always encourage any business to try and do things as sustainably as possible and for the beer industry it should be no different,' he says. 'Technology is constantly evolving to help us use less water etc. Not everyone can be based out in the countryside like us, but there are always ways to ensure you're brewing with a conscience which is something we're great believers in.'

Another aspect of Purity's approach is striving to make organic beer. The company recently received the Soil Association's organic certification process. This is only for Pure Helles, but for Halsey it's another indication of the direction Purity is going.

'For now it is just Pure Helles that has gone organic,' he says, 'and the response has been fantastic. Again for us, it was the right step in the evolution of our business and as previously mentioned brewing with a conscience. There are plans in place to develop this further within our range, but nothing we can announce yet.'

Purity also place great importance on being part of the local community, in their sports' sponsorships for instance – they were recently announced as official ale supplier to Aston Villa, while they also have the first and only Cask Marque accredited beer in a stadium in the UK at Wasps Rugby.

I am an Alcester man,' says Halsey, 'and so the local community has always been integral to the business and remains a key pillar of ours. Many of the brew team are locals who have joined the business and grown with it. The eco-friendly approach has also allowed us to help the local farming community too, with our spent resources and we also support a number of local events where we can.'

Find out more about Purity Brewing at puritybrewing.com

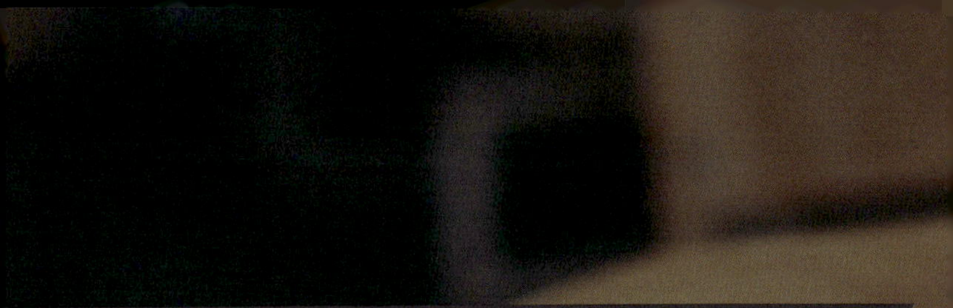

Celebrating Jaipur

The IPA that changed British beer

I was in a pub in Sheffield several months back and it was my round. 'Surprise us,' came the cry from the rest of the table as I asked everyone what they wanted. So I went to the bar, had a look at the taps, which had a weird and wonderful variety of different craft beers, but settled for Thornbridge's Jaipur, which everyone devoured with gusto. Sometimes the best things in life are easy.

Jaipur is a beer I have loved from the first time I tried it back in 2006, entranced by its vibrant and colourful tropical fruitiness on both the nose and palate, and its dry, crisp biscuitiness before the bitter, dry and fruity finish. It has never let me down, whether dispensed from cask or a keg. This is a beer I have always liked to contemplate and study before drinking deeply of it and it is truly one of the most influential beers of the last 15 years. It is an icon and a friend, a craft beer standard and the beginning of a trend, that would spawn a whole host of IPAs, Double IPAs and – probably – Milkshake IPAs (though Jaipur has always had a bright and gleaming clarity about it).

Simon Webster is Thornbridge's Chief Executive Officer and back in 2005, when the beer was first brewed, he recalls tasking the brewers (one of whom was a certain Martin Dickie, later to co-found an outfit called BrewDog) to come up with something different.

'At the time there wasn't anything like Jaipur in the market (hard to believe I know with how commonplace IPAs and DIPAs seem now!), so we wanted to brew an IPA which packed a real punch in terms of both flavour and ABV.

'At that time we had no brewing heritage so we wanted to create something to break the mould. We thought it was a great beer but when the awards started coming in I think it did take us by surprise, from the first gold medal for Beer of the Festival in Sheffield they kept on rolling in. It was when the phones started ringing off the hook with orders that we realised we'd done something pretty special.'

In some ways, this was an international beer. It looked to the US craft beer scene for its marvellously hoppy character, while the name comes from the Indian city with its famous pink walls (which is why the beer's label is the same colour), where Thornbridge founders and owners Jim and Emma Harrison were married.

As Webster says, this was a beer that was very much on its own in 2005, and it has also survived and continues to impress and win awards. 'There are a number of reasons for its survival,' he says, 'for many people who contact us Jaipur was an entry point into the world of beer for them and there is an element of sentimentality to that. I think there is also a lot to be said for quality and consistency, our brewers are incredibly

passionate about the beer and ensuring each and every pint tastes exactly as it should be.'

The hops used are the American varieties Chinook, Centennial, Ahtanum, Simcoe, Columbus and Cascade, which give it that energetic and zesty fruitiness and despite its 5.9% ABV it is an easy drinking beer. It is also a beer that Webster recommends to be drunk young and fresh.

In 2015, Jaipur was joined by Jaipur X, an annually brewed 10% DIPA, which definitely demands to be treated with respect. 'We wanted to brew a beer to celebrate our 10th anniversary,' says Webster, 'so really it had to be a Jaipur related beer and it had to be 10%! It's an absolutely smashing beer and it sneaks up on you a little – we still have people asking for it year after year which is testament I think to how good it is.'

Jaipur: so good they named it twice...

Other Midlands IPAs to look out for whilst in the region:

- Black Iris Circle of Snakes, 8%
- Buxton Axe Edge, 6.8%
- Heritage Brewing Masterpiece IPA, 5.6%
- Neon Raptor Evil Unicorns, 6.3%

By Adrian Tierney-Jones

THORNBRID
B
T

A 33-mile beer adventure

The Black Country Tap Tour

Starting just over two miles north of central Wolverhampton and finishing right next to Kidderminster train station The Black Country Brewery Tap Tour is a challenge for adventurous beer-lovers who want to sample some of the best beers in the region right at their source.

The Black Country has long been synonymous with good beer, thanks to ever-present traditional breweries in the region such as Bathams and Holden's, and now more recently with the arrival of Green Duck Beer Co (pg. 81) and Beat Brewery (pg. 69). There is a charming vibrancy about beer in this region and if you're feeling gutsy and thirsty, then why not embark on a 33-mile sip savouring trip which carves a back-to-front 'S' shape right through the heart of the Black Country. There will be plenty of beers to taste, from milds to double IPAs, and even more stories to uncover along the way.

Ranging from Hail to the Ale in the North to The Weavers Real Ale House in the South at Kidderminster, this trip, with the right amount of preparation and investigation of public transport, can be done in a day or perhaps it's better achieved, or enjoyed, over a weekend!

Start your perambulation with Hail to the Ale (hailtothealemicropub.co.uk), a corner micropub belonging to Morton Brewery. There are usually four cask beers on, with at least one from Morton, while bar snacks include pies, cheese, sausage rolls and Scotch eggs.

The Waggon & Horses in Tipton has long been a favourite for the beer tourist, partly because it always has seven cask beers on and also because since 2004 it has been the home of Toll End Brewery, whose beers are at the bar along with guests.

Next stop is the Park Inn (holdensbrewery.co.uk/pubs) in Woodsetton, Dudley. The pub is right next to Holden's Brewery and regularly serves four of its beers, including its Black Country Mild, a traditional beer of the area. Food is also served (but not on Sundays) and it can get busy as the day wears on.

Next on your tour is the historic Beacon Hotel (sarahhughesbrewery.co.uk) in Sedgley, Dudley, the home of Sarah Hughes Brewery, famous for its 5.9% Dark Ruby Mild. Built in the 19th century, this is a solid-looking building with a redbrick tower brewery at the back.

Now let's take a trip to the Jolly Crispin, the home of Fownes Brewing. This has been a pub for 200 years and as well as featuring beers from its parent brewery, other regulars include Oakham's Bishop's Farewell.

We're remaining in Dudley for a visit to The Old Bulls Head (blackcountryales.co.uk/pubs/old-bulls-head), owned by Black Country Ales. An attractive looking redbrick Victorian-era pub, this is also the home of Black Country Ales and its beers naturally feature at the bar-top.

In 1974, the Old Swan Inn was one of the last four remaining brewpubs in the UK (and also known as Ma Pardoe's). There was an interregnum in brewing between 1988 and 2001, but the brewhouse is kept busy these days with five of its beers regularly available at the atmospheric pub. A real historical gem.

The Fixed Wheel Tap House (fixedwheelbrewery.co.uk/visit-us) can be found in Blackheath, where there are 10 keg and six cask beers available. Dog and child-friendly, it is open weekends and the brewing team are usually on hand for those interested in the process.

Opened in 2019, the Beat Brewery (pg. 69) Taphouse is next door to Sadler's Brewhouse and more significantly only a stone's throw from Lye train station. This makes it a reasonable place to start or finish if you can't complete the whole tour. The light and airy modern taphouse has keg, cask and bottles available but is only open on Fridays and Saturdays.

Originally home to a brewery of the same name from 1900-27, the Windsor Castle Inn was where Sadler's Ales (pg. 86) begun brewing in 2004 before moving to their new brewhouse, also in Lye. However, with a member of the Sadler family running the inn, this is a place to drink deeply of their beers.

It might lack Victorian fittings and a history going back to the days of Moses, but Green Duck Brew Co's (pg. 81) Badelynge Bar (greenduckbrewery.co.uk/visit-us) is an excellent laid-back place to sample their freshest beers. Note, open at weekends only.

Craddock's Brewery call The Duke William in Stourbridge home, a lovely looking redbrick corner pub with a cosy interior. Craddock's beers are naturally available, along with guests, while brewery tours can be arranged in advance.

Batham'ss is a well-loved Black Country brewery and you can sample its Mild and Best Bitter right next to the brewery at The Vine Inn, or Bull & Bladder as it's known locally (bathams.co.uk/pubs/the-vine-inn). This is a real community pub, with several rooms including a snug, lounge and back bar.

The final stop of the Black Country Brewery Tap Tour is The Weavers Real Ale House in Kidderminster, where Pig Iron Brewery's beers are available, alongside a sparkling selection from other Midlands breweries. A one-room pub, comfortable and cosy, where conversation and beer are the order of the day.

Four essential beers to taste whilst exploring the Black Country Brewery Tap Tour:

- Sarah Hughes, Dark Ruby Mild
- Batham's, Bitter
- Black Country Ales, Fireside Bitter
- Green Duck, One Great Thing Pale Ale

Highlights
Established: 1995
Beers produced: 15
DRINK
SHOP

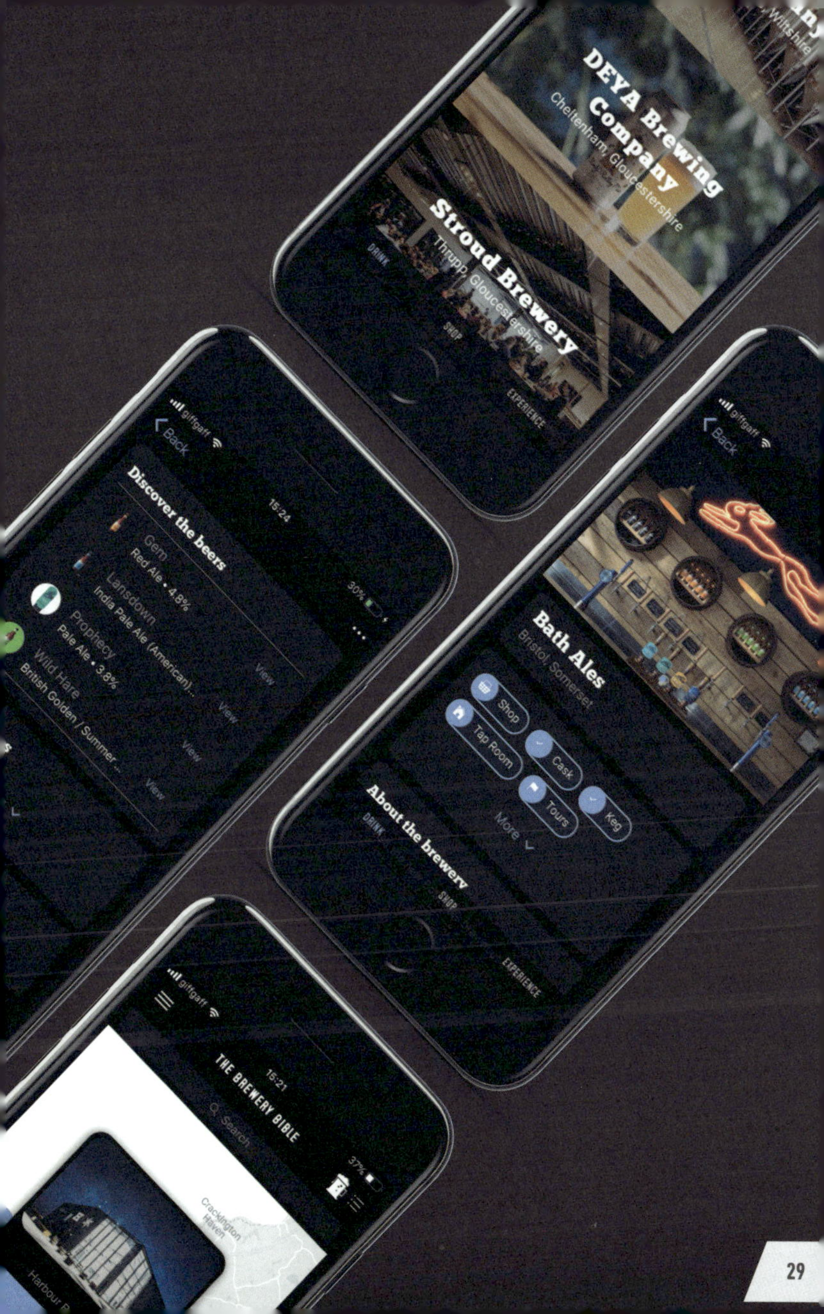
DEYA Brewing Company
Cheltenham, Gloucestershire
Stroud Brewery
Thrupp, Gloucestershire
DRINK
SHOP
EXPERIENCE
giffgaff
Back
15:24
30%
Discover the beers
Gem
Red Ale • 4.8%
View
Lansdown
India Pale Ale (American)...
View
Prophecy
Pale Ale • 3.8%
View
Wild Hare
British Golden / Summer...
View
giffgaff
Back
Bath Ales
Bristol, Somerset
Shop
Cask
Tap Room
Tours
Keg
More
About the brewery
DRINK
SHOP
EXPERIENCE
giffgaff
15:21
THE BREWERY BIBLE
Search
37%
Crackington Haven

The following guide includes information on over 200 Midlands breweries, as well as an in-depth look at some of the region's best breweries, beer venues and bottleshops. Organised into county sections to make your next beer adventure in the Midlands super easy to navigate and plan.

All the featured breweries are highlighted on the county maps using their page number. So flick through, discover your next favourite brewery and unravel an endless amount of great tasting beer - whether it's a famous Midlands Mild or a hop forward IPA bursting out of a new tap room, there is bound to be something that tickles your tastebuds.

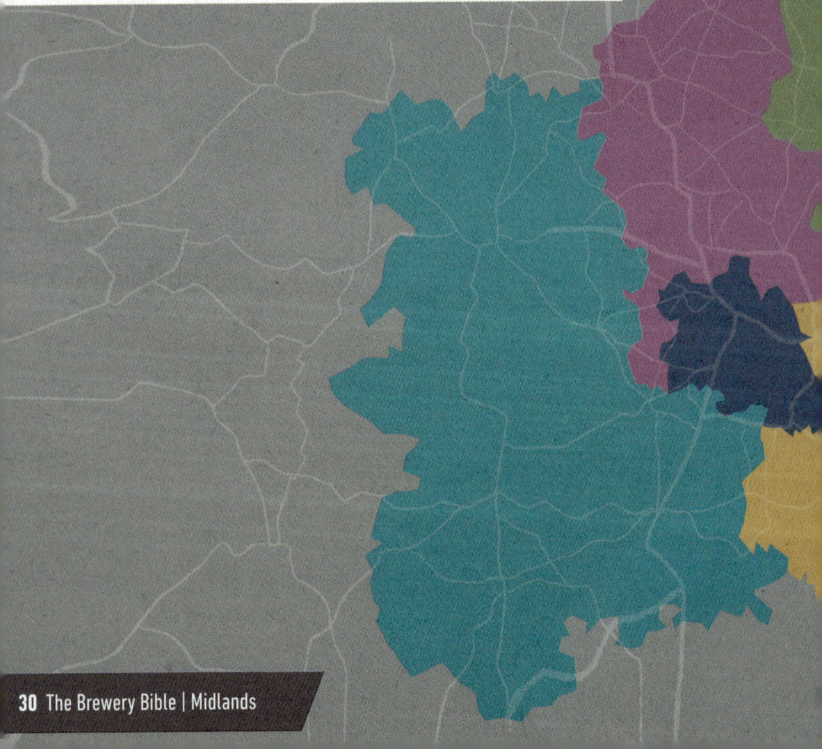

P32 East Midlands

P60 West Midlands

P96 Warwickshire & Northamptonshire

P114 Staffordshire

P134 Herefordshire, Worcestershire & Shropshire

East Midlands

Key

#1 Black Iris Brewery (P34)
#2 Blue Monkey Brewing (P36)
#3 Buxton Brewery (P38)
#4 Charnwood Brewery (P40)
#5 Lincoln Green Brewing Company (P42)
#6 Peak Ales (P44)
#7 The Langton Brewery (P46)
#8 Thornbridge Brewery (P48)
● East Midlands breweries (P56)

#1 Black Iris Brewery

Unit 1, 27 Shipstone Street, Nottingham, Nottinghamshire NG7 6GJ
blackirisbrewery@gmail.com | 07816 148913
@blackiris.brewery @blackirisbrewery @BlackIrisBrewer

About the brewery

There's a vibrancy about Black Iris, which originally started life in 2011 in Derby at the Flowerpot and moved to Nottingham in 2014, where beer is made in the shadow of Shipstone's tower brewery, whose closure in 1991 brought to an end 150 years of brewing.

It could be their stark, monochrome branding that helps the beers stand out on the shelves or at the bar-top, or it might be beer names such as Gimme Fruit, Gimme Fire, Give Me That Which I Papaya or Drink Beer Hail Satan. None of this on its own would be enough though unless the beers showed a corresponding quality and excitement and they certainly do. 'We brew beers with passion, quality ingredients and a punk rock aesthetic courtesy of our excellent designer Kev Grey,' says co-owner Alex Wilson.

The brewery is certainly not afraid to experiment either as a Blueberry IPA filled with blueberry juice, Mosaic and El Dorado hops, Madagascan vanilla beans and lactose milk sugar demonstrated and it also has a barrel-aging program. Occasional events have also taken place at the brewery, notably a metal and beer evening, though the lack of space is prohibitive, probably meaning that Black Iris will have to expand in the near future, which is certainly good news for Nottingham beer-lovers.

Signature brew

Snake Eyes, 3.8%
Fresh and fruity pale ale that makes use of Citra and Cascade hop varieties. This was the first beer Black Iris brewed on moving to Nottingham and has won them several awards.

Established: 2011
Litres per year: 237,000
Brewery tours: No
Taphouse: No
Beers produced: 40
Open: By appoinment only

Established: 2008
Litres per year: 450,000

Brewery tours: Yes
Taphouse: Yes
Beers produced: 30

Open:
Mon - Sat,
9am - 4.30pm

#2 Blue Monkey Brewery

10 Pentrich Road, Giltbrook Industrial Park, Giltbrook, Nottinghamshire NG16 2UZ
bluemonkeybrewery.com | sales@bluemonkeybrewery.com | 01159 385899
@bluemonkeybrewery @bluemonkeybrew @bluemonkeybrew

About the brewery

Eleven years have passed since Blue Monkey was founded in the town of Ilkeston, with its name coming from the iron works that used to be based in the town – when the furnaces were fired up, two blue flames used to appear and reach towards the sky, which were nicknamed by the locals as 'blue monkeys'. There's a further link: the grandfather of the founder used to work at the foundry making the brewery's name a tender memorial to the now sadly departed man.

The aim of the brewery is simple: 'We aim to brew exceptional beers for beer drinking enthusiasts and newcomers alike and have a selection of quirky named beers to excite the customer and delight the drinker. We have a fresh yet traditional approach to our customers creating brews which appeal to all ages.'

Seven regular beers, including the multi-award winning pale ale BG Sips, the luscious stout Guerilla and the well-hopped strong pale ale Ape Ale, are produced, while there are also seasonal and special brews. The brewery also has four comfortable and popular pubs, which are branded the Organ Grinder (pg. 54); these can be found in Nottingham, Loughborough, Newark and Arnold, while there is also a mobile bar. As if this wasn't enough, Blue Monkey also have several Blue Monkey gins in different flavours.

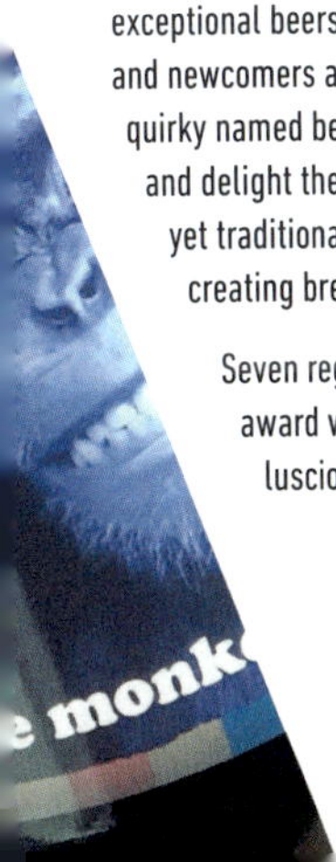

Signature brew

Infinity IPA, 4.6%
Massive amounts of the classic hop Citra are added to this glittering golden ale, giving it a big boost of tropical fruit on the nose and palate, alongside a dry bittersweet finish. Champion golden ale of Great Britain in 2017.

#3 Buxton Brewery

Buxton Brewery, Unit 4a/4b Staden Lane, Staden, Buxton, Derbyshire SK17 9RZ
buxtonbrewery.co.uk | contact@buxtonbrewery.co.uk | 01298 24420
@BuxtonBreweryCompany @buxtonbrewery @buxtonbrewery

About the brewery

Buxton opened in 2009 and was one of the brewing stars of the wave of craft breweries that emerged around the start (or just a year or so on each side) of the current decade and included The Kernel and Magic Rock. Geoff Quinn is the founder and he moved to the Peak District in 2002 so he could be close to world class climbing. 'The original ethos and brewery mission is still standing,' he says. 'It's a simple one, we strive to make the best beer possible, always with high-drinkability, no matter what the style is, whether sours, IPAs, simple bitters or complex imperial stouts. There isn't much more to it than that really. Maintaining and staying true to this ethos is the real trick – never to become complacent, or think that we've mastered any aspect of brewing.'

The first beer to be brewed was Buxton SPA, a 4.1% well-hopped pale ale, which is still part of the brewery's core range and one of its best selling beers. Other beers in the core range include Axe Edge and Moor Top, but as Quinn says, 'we still love to experiment, and with that experimentation we've invented new techniques (or techniques we haven't come across before) and completely new beer styles'.

Signature brew

Axe Edge, 6.8%
Described as a 'relentless hoppy IPA' and first brewed in 2011, this is a furnace wave blast of tropical fruit on the nose with more fruit on the palate and a dry finish.

Established: 2008
Litres per year: 500,000

Brewery tours: Coming Soon
Taphouse: Yes, see pg 51

Beers produced: 30 different beers anually

Established: 2014
Litres per year: 330,000
Brewery tours: No
Taphouse: Yes
Beers produced: 40
Open: See website

#4 Charnwood Brewery

22 Jubilee Drive, Loughborough, Leicestershire LE11 5XS
charnwoodbrewery.co.uk | hello@charnwoodbrewery.co.uk | 01509 218666
@Charnwoodbrewery @Charnwood_brewery @charnbrew

About the brewery

Localism has become an important issue for many brewers. Consumers want local beers, as they want locally produced food, and this consideration was a key factor for Andrew and Andrea Reed when they opened Charnwood in 2014 in their home town of Loughborough in the middle of the Charnwood Hills. Andrew had worked in the brewing/pub business for 25 years, though Andrea's background was nursing, sales, PR, and data analysis. Undaunted she went for a nine-month apprenticeship under the guidance of Brewsters Brewery. Their combined experience and drive all seems to have worked as the brewery has won several National SIBA (Society of Independent Brewers) gold medals.

Returning to localism, the brewery sells 99% of its beer within 15 miles of the brewery, focusing its sales on three main brands: the cask beers Salvation (3.8%), Vixen (4%) and the pale hoppy 'craft' keg beer American Pale Ale (4.8%). Throughout the year, these are supplemented by a series of seasonal beers in cask, bottle, and keg. You can get a sense and a feel for the mood of Charnwood by visiting their lively shop and tap room where locals drink the beers yards from where they are made. The brewery also opened its first micro-pub in the nearby village of Mountsorrel last November and have plans for more in the Charnwood Hills. Local is the new global perhaps?

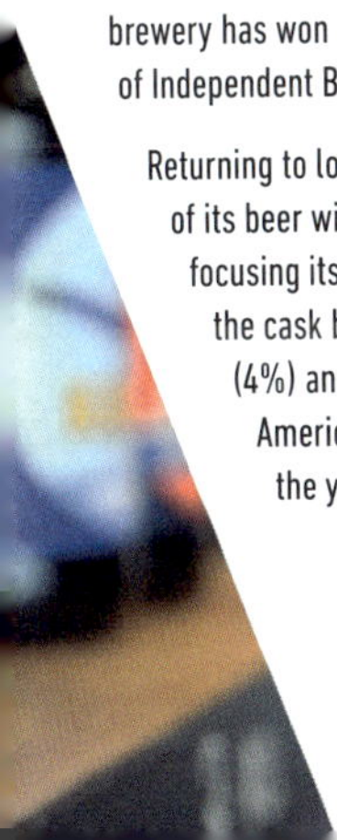

Signature brew

APA, 4.8%

The Reeds are big fans of the American pale ale style and their version uses four classic US hops (Cascade, Centennial, Citra and Chinook), which impart a citrus aroma with a robust fruity bitterness.

#5 Lincoln Green Brewing Company

Unit E5 Enterprise Park, Wigwam Lane, Hucknall, Nottinghamshire NG15 7SZ
lincolngreenbrewing.co.uk | contact@lincolngreenbrewing.co.uk | 01159 634233
@LGBCLTD @LincolnGBrewing @LincolnGBrewing

About the brewery

Lincoln Green started brewing in the town of Hucknall in 2012, with the name coming from the colour of dyed woollen clothes worn by Robin Hood, 'and like Robin Hood we believe in putting people at the heart of everything we do. Furthermore, by knowing that every sip and visit is important our multi-award winning ales and pubs are becoming legends in their own right'. You might want to try a pint of the 4% American Pale Archer, which is packed with Chinook and Citra hops, or how about the multi-award winning Tuck Porter at 4.7%.

The brewery also owns five pubs in and around Hucknall, as well as in Nottingham, where the Sir John Borlase Warren has one of the best beer gardens in the city. 'Lincoln Green pubs are timeless spaces that are at the heart of the neighbourhood they serve. They look to reflect the modern day values of George Orwell's The Moon Under Water essay from the Evening Standard in which he described his vision of the perfect pub.'

With people remaining at the heart of Lincoln Green's approach, the company also helps local communities with weekly meat raffles that raise money for local causes, cider pressings that increase awareness of post-traumatic stress syndrome and Combat Stress, and beer festivals that raise much needed funds for Air Ambulance and CLIC Sargent.

Signature brew

Archer American Pale Ale, 4%
Plenty of colourful and vibrant American hops are packed into this fruity and bittersweet APA, making it punch far above its 4% ABV.

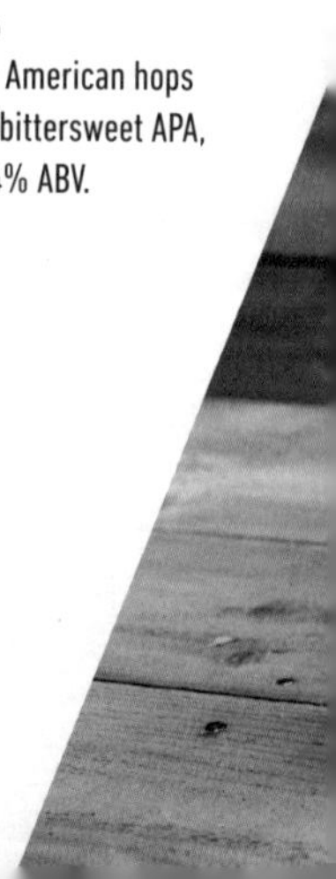

Established: 2012
Litres per year: 300,000
Brewery tours: No
Taphouse: Yes - The Station Hotel, Hucknall
Beers produced: 20
Open: Brewery - Mon - Fri 9am - 5pm

Established: 2005
Litres per year: 400,000

Brewery tours: Yes
Taphouse: Yes
Beers produced: 10

Open: Mon - Sun 11am - 4pm (Plus late night events monthly)

#6 Peak Ales

The Barn Brewery, Chatsworth, Derbyshire DE45 1EX
peakales.co.uk | info@peakales.co.uk | 01246 583737
@peakales @peakales @peakales

About the brewery

When Robert and Debra Evans opened Peak Ales in 2005 in a restored barn on Chatsworth Estate they were following in a longstanding tradition of beer making at stately homes, something Chatsworth had already done in the distant past.

Sales of Peak's beers grew and by 2012 the original home had become too small and so a new 20-barrel plant was moved to a purpose-built premises in Ashford in the Water, still in the Peak District though. The barn? This remained pretty special to the Evans' and they have just completed a brewery visitor centre and gin distillery there, which also includes a 2.5-barrel pilot brewery that allows them to experiment with new recipes and beer styles. It is also obviously somewhere you can go and taste the whole range of Peak Ales, which includes award-winning cask and bottled beers, alongside seasonal specials and experimental brews from the pilot.

There's a heartening symmetry about Peak Ales retaining a presence at Chatsworth especially given its past history as a country house brewery, though what happened then would probably not happen at Peak Ales – a tale is told of when the beer was brewed it was piped to grand carved casks in the cellar. However, some enterprising under-gardeners found the pipe, drilled a hole and stuck a plug in it so they could fill their buckets on brewing day!

Signature brew

Chatsworth Gold, 4.6%
Golden ale made with honey collected from the Chatsworth Estate. Expect a delicate sweetness, well balanced with bitterness from the classic English hop partnership of Goldings and Fuggles.

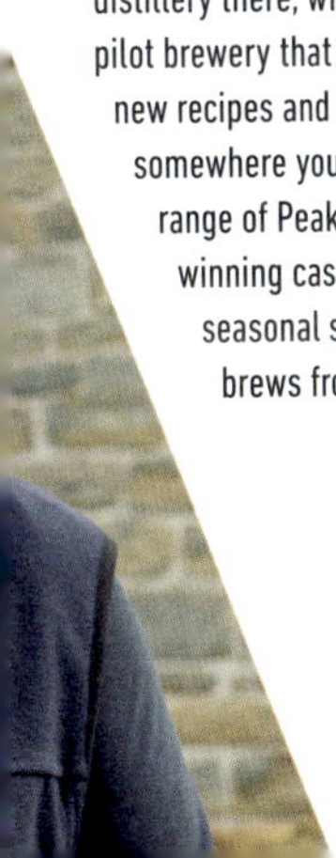

#7 Langton Brewery

Grange Farm, Welham Rd, Thorpe Langton, Market Harborough, Leicestershire LE16 7TU
langtonbrewery.co.uk | info@langtonbrewery.co.uk | 01858 540116
@langton.brewery @langtonbrewery @langtonbrewery

About the brewery

In 2019 Langton celebrates 20 years as a brewery. It started life at the back of the Bell Inn, East Langton, where the beer was brewed for the pub and the local cricket team. With a new team in place since 2017 Langton is in an exciting stage of its journey and the popularity of their beers continues to grow as exciting new releases like the West Coast IPA 'Jabber' and craft lager 'Chinwag' as well as award winning traditional ales are being produced.

'We are a small independent business. No one else influences the beers we brew. We only craft beers we want to brew and like to drink. To us, producing craft beer is about having a direct influence and control over all the ingredients throughout our brewery process. We have minimal automation - each day our brewers handle, smell and taste our raw ingredients.'

We love being part of the local fabric in a beautiful, hidden spot in Leicestershire's Welland Valley and are excited about the challenge of making new, interesting and innovative beers as the beer market in the Midlands develops."

Signature brew

Inclined Plane, 4.2%

A refreshing amber-coloured bitter with a light floral finish, while the late addition of the Amarillo hop instils a distinct citrus flavour. First brewed in 2004, this is a multi-award winning beer and named after the canal boat lift operating in the 1900s at the Foxton Locks in Leicestershire.

Established: 1999
Litres per year: 200,000

Brewery tours: Yes
Taphouse: Opening Spring 2020

Beers produced: 23
Open: Mon - Fri 8am - 4pm

Established: 2005
Litres per year: 360,0000
Brewery tours: Yes
Taphouse: Yes
Beers produced: 250
Open: Mon - Tues 9am - 5pm, Weds - Thurs 9am - 6pm, Fri 9am - 8pm & Sat 10am - 8pm

#8 Thornbridge Brewery

Riverside Brewery, Buxton Rd, Bakewell, Derbyshire DE45 1GS
thornbridgebrewery.co.uk | info@thornbridge.co.uk | 01629 815999
@thornbridgebrewery @thornbridge @thornbridge

About the brewery

Trail-blazers, trend-setters, innovators and boundary-pushers – Thornbridge is all of these and yet it has never forgotten its core values of quality and consistency, which has helped it create an award-winning range of beers that has won fans across the world.

Founded in 2005 and initially brewing at Thornbridge Hall, it moved to its state-of-the-art brewery in 2009, a hub of activity that also houses its popular brewery tap. Tours can be booked, a well-made learning experience that takes in a forest of stainless steel as well as rows of wooden barrels where various beers mature and sleep the sleep of the just.

Jaipur is the beer that everyone knows (see page 20), but there is also St Petersburg's imperial stout, the juicy pale ale Crackendale and the unctuous Necessary Evil, a 13% bourbon barrel-aged stout that is only available in bottle. The brewery also has a selection of pubs, such as the Bath Hotel in Sheffield, and once a year at the Bakewell Showground, it holds Peakender, a festival of music, talks, meet the brewer events and, above all, a selection of beers from its own brewery and some of the best breweries in the UK. Not for nothing, can Thornbridge be seen as the godparents of the British craft beer scene.

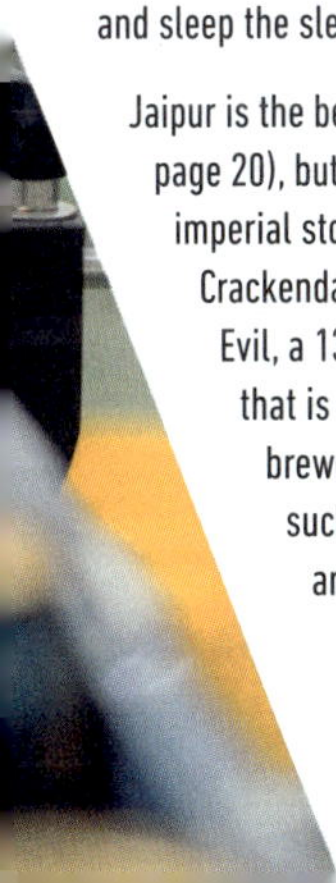

Signature brew

Jaipur, 5.9%
Award winning India Pale Ale packed with hops that was unlike anything in the British beer industry at the time of its release in 2005. Smooth at the start and then building up to a crescendo of massive hoppiness accentuated by honeyed notes.

#9 Brewhouse & Kitchen Sutton Coldfield

The Cup, 8 Birmingham Rd, Sutton Coldfield, Staffordshire B72 1QD
brewhouseandkitchen.com | suttoncoldfield@brewhouseandkitchen.com | 01217 966838
@BKSuttonC @brewhouse_and_kitchen @bksuttonc

About the venue

Originally a pub called The Cup and afterwards briefly a restaurant, Brewhouse & Kitchen opened in Sutton Coldfield in 2015, offering locals core and seasonal craft beers brewed onsite, plus a further selection of beers from well-regarded breweries. Inside, there's a bright and vibrant ambience, and outside there's a comfortable beer garden which includes a fire pit, pizza oven shack and 15-litre serve-yourself keg tables and outdoor games. Unique beer experiences offered include having a go at brewing under the guidance of the head brewer and a regular Beer Masterclass.

Mission statement

Inspired by the craft beer movement in the USA, Brewhouse & Kitchen Sutton Coldfield belongs to the largest brewpub group in the UK (and the second largest in Europe!). Our founders Kris and Simon created Brewhouse & Kitchen as a craft beer and brewing offering for everyone and it was very important from the start that Brewhouse & Kitchen would push the barriers in the pub industry and continue to raise the game in the world of beer.

Open: Sun - Thu 11am - 11pm, Fri - Sat 11am - midnight
Established: 2015

No. of beers sold: 50+ craft beers & a range of beers brewed on-site
Takeout: No

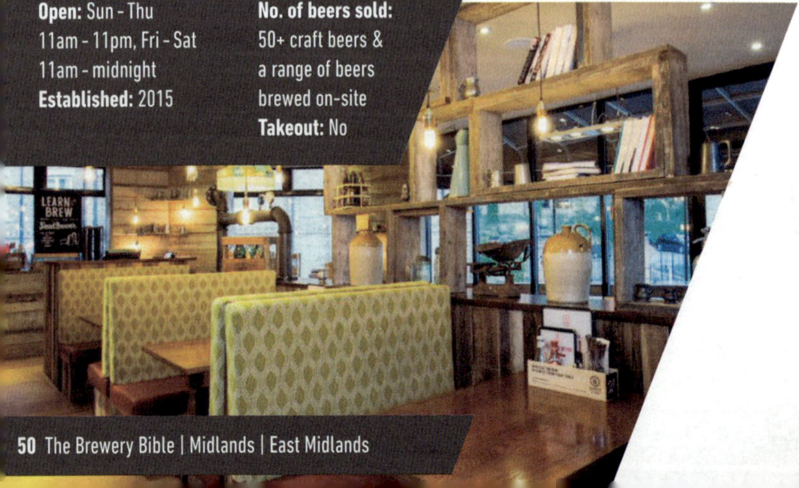

Open:
Mon-Thurs
midday - 11.30pm,
Fri 12pm - 00.30am,
Sat 11am - 00.30am,
Sun 11am - 23.30pm
Established: 2013

No. of beers sold:
Tap House, 16 Keg Taps and 2 Cask Taps. Cellar Bar, 12 Keg Taps and 2 Cask Taps
Takeout: Yes

#10 Buxton Brewery Tap House & Cellar

The Old Court House, George Street, Buxton, Derbyshire SK17 6AY
buxtonbrewery.co.uk/tap-house | contact@buxtontaphouse.co.uk | 01298 214085
@BuxtonTapHouse @buxtontaphouse @buxtontaphouse

About the venue

Lucky old Buxton, not only is it home to the eponymous brewery, but 2013 saw the opening of the Tap House & Cellar, where local beer-lovers fell immediately in love with the brewery's beers as well as a diverse range of beers from around the world. This is also the place to be to try Buxton's latest and freshest new releases before they go out into the trade. As well as the beer, there is an appetising and enticing selection of dishes with lots of home-smoked meat on the menu.

Mission statement

Buxton Brewery has three venues; Tap House, Cellar and Tasting Room - all with one aim, to have dedicated spaces to showcase the brewery's beers as well as those produced by our favourite craft breweries across the globe in a relaxed setting. We hope you have fun exploring Buxton and our welcoming bars!

#11 Hopology

126 Melton Road, West Bridgford, Nottinghamshire NG2 6EP
hopology.uk | nick@hopology.co.uk | 01159 816346
@HopologyBeerShop @hopologybeer

About the venue

You will find Hopology in West Bridgford, just south of Nottingham. Time is needed to browse through its selection of beers, that include products from excellent local breweries such as Black Iris and Neon Raptor and others further afield in the UK and Europe. Its dedication to excellence has also been recognised with several awards including the winner in the Off License News Midlands Region independent beer retailer. Also, keep an eye out for occasional meet the brewer nights.

Mission statement

In addition to an extensive selection of the best British craft beer we endeavour to stock a wide range of European beers. The Belgian beers are particularly special to us and we have always tried to support some of the best smaller breweries from that country, especially those producing some of the rarer lambics.

Open: Mon - Sun
11am - 7pm (Check website for weekday variations)

Established: 2013
No. of beers sold: 400
Sit-in: No

Open: Everyday 10am - midnight
Established: 2016

No. of beers sold: 12 keg, 6 cask & 100+ bottles/cans
Takeout: Yes

#12 Six Barrel Drafthouse

14/16 Carlton Street, Nottingham, Nottinghamshire NG1 1NN
sixbarreldrafthouse.co.uk | info@sixbarreldrafthouse.co.uk | 01159 501798
@SixBarrelDrafthouse @sixbarreldrafthousehockley @SixBarrelDraft

About the venue

If there was such a thing as time travel you could go back to 1874 and be present at the opening of what was then called the Lord Nelson pub, but now you visit to take in the sensitively modern conversion, the excellent range of keg and cask beers (including the likes of Black Iris and Liquid Light) and a warm welcome from pub dog Ginnie.

Locally roasted '200 Degrees' coffee is served from 10am daily, regular mini beer festivals and beer launches are held, and the Drafthouse always takes part in Nottingham's Craft Beer Week in June.

Mission statement

To always offer a friendly and welcoming city centre bar atmosphere, with an excellent choice of beer and a passion for all things beer, gin, music and good times.

As well as one of the best ranges of craft beer in the city we cater for gin lovers, whisky and rum fans as well as lager and cider drinkers. We're a cosy and warm pub, super dog friendly with pop-up street food events happening all the time.

#13 The Organ Grinder, Nottingham

21 Alfreton Road, Nottingham, Nottinghamshire NG7 3JE
bluemonkeybrewery.com | sales@bluemonkeybrewery.com | 01159 700630
@OGnotts @organgrinder.notts

About the venue

The aim of the Organ Grinder (which is one of several Blue Monkey Brewery pubs) is to create an atmosphere of comfort and cosiness, where the brewery's beers, as well as two real ciders and one perry, can be enjoyed. During cooler seasons, the wood-burning fire rivals the solid bar as an eye-catching centre of attention, while in warmer weather do venture outside to the rear and up a few steps where you will find a city centre oasis of calm on the roof terrace.

Mission statement

Once called The Red Lion, this was bought and refurbished by Blue Monkey and it is the brewery tap-house, where the fullest range of our beers can be found anywhere in the world. Our aim in this single-roomed pub is to get people to relax and just enjoy themselves. We also run an after work perk Friday (5-8pm), which include all cask beer and Blue Monkey lager for just £3 per pint. Bargain!

Open:
Sun - Wed 12pm - 11pm,
Thurs 12pm - 11.30pm,
Fri - Sat 12pm - 12am

Established: 2011
No. of beers sold:
9 cask 8 kegs beers
Takeout: Yes

Open: Mon - Tues 9am - 5pm, Wed - Thurs 9am - 6pm, Fri 9am - 8pm Sat - 10am-8pm

Established: 2005

No. of beers sold: 30

Takeout: Yes

#14 Thornbridge Taproom

Riverside Brewery, Buxton Rd, Bakewell Derbyshire DE45 1GS
thornbridgebrewery.co.uk | info@thornbridge.co.uk | 01629 815994
@thornbridgebrewery @thornbridgetap @thornbridgetap

About the venue

From the outside, massive windows reveal a vast thicket of shining brewing equipment, where Thornbridge's brewers weave their magic spells, and right next door is the tap room, rustic and cosy in its interior ambience and a place to drink great beers at their source with eight keg lines and two cask, plus bottles, cans and a range of merch. Regular brewery tours happen every Wednesday, Thursday and Friday at 1pm and 3pm, while brewery socials are always on the last Wednesday and Saturday of the month.

Mission statement

Serving brewery fresh beer, right at the source. Thornbridge Taproom is situated right next to the main brewhouse and the tap room itself doubles as our barrel-ageing room. We love the fact that you can drink the same beers in the very same space they were created.

East Midlands Breweries

8 Sail Brewery 4 Hale Rd, Heckington, Sleaford, Lincolnshire NG34 9JW | 01529 469308
8sailbrewery.co.uk

Abstract Jungle Brewery Unit 1, Baileybrook Industrial Estate, Langley Mill, Nottinghamshire NG16 4BE | 07481 849332
abstractjunglebrewery.co.uk

Aldwark Artisan Ales Lydgate Farm, Aldwark, Matlock, Derbyshire DE4 4HW | 01629 540720
aaabrewery.co.uk

All Saints Brewery & Pub 21-22 All Saints St, Stamford, Lincolnshire PE9 2PA | 01937 832225
allsaintsbrewery.co.uk

Amber Ales Unit 7, Outram Business Centre, Whiteley Rd, Ripley, Derbyshire DE5 3QL
01773 512864 | amberales.co.uk

Anstey Ale Brewery 46A Albion St, Anstey, Leicester, Leicestershire LE7 7DE
07960 776843 | ansteyale.co.uk

Ashover Brewery Unit 1, Kershaw Buildings, Derby Rd Business Pk, Clay Cross, Derbyshire S45 9AG | 01246 251859
ashoverbrewery.co.uk

Aurora Ales Gallows Industrial Estate Unit 6, Furnace Rd, Ilkeston, Derbyshire DE7 5EP
07768 976999 | aurora-ales.co.uk

Bad Ram Brewery Callow Top Holiday Park, Buxton Road, Sandybrook, Ashbourne, Derbyshire DE6 2AQ | 01335 344020
ww.badrambrewery.co.uk

Baker's Dozen Brewing Co Unit 5 Ketton Business Park, Pit Lane, Stamford, Lincolnshire PE9 3SZ | 01780 238180
bakersdozenbrewing.co.uk

Bang The Elephant Brewing Co Unit 14, Bailey Brook Business Industrial Estate, Amber Drive, Langley Mill, Derbyshire NG16 4BE
07976 913395

Batemans Brewery Salem Bridge Brewery, Mill Ln, Wainfleet All Saints, Skegness, Lincolnshire PE24 4JE | 01754 880317
bateman.co.uk

Beermats Brewing Company New Yard, Newark, Nottinghamshire NG22 8PQ | 01636 639004
beermatsbeer.co.uk

Belvoir Brewery Crown Park, Station Rd, Old Dalby, Melton Mowbray, Leicestershire LE14 3NQ
01664 823455 | belvoirbrewery.co.uk

Black Hole Brewery Unit 3a, Old Hall Mill Business Park Alfreton Rd, Little Eaton, Derbyshire DE21 5EJ | 01283 619943
blackholebrewery.co.uk

**Black Iris Brewery Unit 1, Shipstone St, Nottingham, Nottinghamshire NG7 6GJ
01159 791936
facebook.com/blackiris.brewery**

**Blue Monkey Brewery 10 Pentrich Rd/Giltbrook Ind. Park, Nottingham, Nottinghamshire NG16 2UZ
01159 385899 | bluemonkeybrewery.com**

Boot Brewery (The Boot Inn) 12 Boot Hill, Repton, Derbyshire DE65 6FT | 01283 346047
thebootatrepton.co.uk

Brampton Brewery Units 4 & 5, Chatsworth Business Park, Chatsworth Road, Chesterfield, Derbyshire S40 2AS | 01246 221680
bramptonbrewery.co.uk

Brewster's Brewing Co 5 Burnside, Turnpike Close, Grantham, Lincolnshire NG31 7XU
01476 566000 | brewstersbrewery.com

Brunswick Brewing Company 1 Railway Terrace, Derbyshire DE1 2RU | 01332 410055 brunswickbrewingcompany.co.uk

Buxton Brewery Unit 4A & 4B, Staden Lane, Staden, Buxton, Derbyshire SK17 9RZ 01298 244200 | buxtonbrewery.co.uk

Castle Rock Brewery Queensbridge Rd, Nottingham, Nottinghamshire NG2 1NB 01159 851 615 | castlerockbrewery.co.uk

Charnwood Brewery 22 Jubilee Drive, Loughborough, Leicestershire LE11 5XS 01509 218666 | charnwoodbrewery.co.uk

Co Pilot Brewery Unit 4, Sam Brown Industrial Units, Dog & Gun Lane, Whetstone, Leicester, Leicestershire LE8 6LJ | 07897 895511

Dancing Duck Brewery John Cooper Buildings, Payne Street, Derbyshire DE22 3AZ | 01332 205582 dancingduckbrewery.com

Derby Brewing Company Masons Place Business Park, 11 Nottingham Rd, Derbyshire DE21 6AQ 01332 365366 | derbybrewing.co.uk

Derventio Brewery Darley Abbey Mills, The Brew Shed, Darley Abbey, Derbyshire DE22 1DZ 01332 380199 | derventiobrewery.co.uk

Double Top Brewery 4, Kilton Terrace, Bracebridge, Worksop, Nottinghamshire S80 2DY 07973 521 824 | doubletopbrewery.co.uk

Dovedale Brewing Company Damgate Farm, Ilam, Nr Ashbourne, Derbyshire DE6 2AD | 01335 310271 dovedalebrewing.co.uk

Dow Bridge Brewery 2-3 Rugby Road, Lutterworth, Leicestershire LE17 6DA | 01788 869121 dowbridgebrewery.co.uk

Drone Valley Brewery Unit 2, Unstone Industrial Complex, Main Rd, Dronfield, Derbyshire S18 4AB 07794 277091 | dronevalleybrewery.com

Dukeries Brewery 6 Woodland Drive, Worksop, Nottinghamshire S81 0TP | 01909 731171 dukeriesbrewery.co.uk

Elmesthorpe Brewery Church Farm, Station Road, Elmesthorpe, Leicestershire LE9 7SG 07754 321283 | elmesthorpebrewery.co.uk

Everards of Leicestershire Optimus Point, Devana Avenue, Glenfield, Leicestershire LE3 8JS 01162 014100 | everards.co.uk

Ferry Ales Brewery Ferry Rd, Lincoln, Lincolnshire LN3 4HU | 0800 999 3226 ferryalesbrewery.co.uk

Firehouse Brewery 3-7 Thames St, Louth, Lincolnshire LN11 7AD | 01507 608202 firehouse-brewery.co.uk

Flash Brewery Buxton, Derbyshire SK17 0SY 07967 592345 | flashbrewery.uk

Framework Brewery The Old City Depot, 72-74 Friday St, Leicester, Leicestershire LE1 3BW 01162 624037 | frameworkbrewery.com

Golden Duck Brewery Unit 2, Red Hill Farm, Appleby Magna, Swadlincote, Leicestershire DE12 7AH | 07427 403328 goldenduckbrewery.com

Grafton Brewing Co Walters Yard, Dukeries Way, Claylands Industrial Estate, Worksop, Nottinghamshire S81 7DW | 01909 476 121 graftonbrewing.co.uk

Grainstore Brewery Station Approach, Oakham, Rutland LE15 6RE | 01572 770065 grainstorebrewery.com

Grasshopper Brewery Langley Mill, Eastwood, Nottingham, Nottinghamshire NG16 3RZ 01773 530 224 | grasshopperbrewery.co.uk

Hartshorns Brewery Unit 4, Tomlinsons Industrial Estate, Alfreton Rd, Derbyshire DE21 4ED 07830 367125 | hartshornsbrewery.com

Hopshackle Brewery Unit F, Bentley Business Park, Blenheim Way, Northfields Industrial Estate, Market Deeping, Lincolnshire PE6 8LD 07894 348542 | hopshacklebrewery.co.uk

East Midlands Breweries

Horncastle Ales (Old Nicks Tavern) 8 North St, Horncastle, Lincolnshire LN9 5DX | 01507 526862

Howard Town Brewery Hope St, Glossop, Derbyshire SK13 7SS | 01457 869800 howardtownbrewery.co.uk

Kings Clipstone Brewery Main Road, Kings Clipstone, Mansfield, Nottinghamshire NG21 9BT 01623 823 589 | kingsclipstonebrewery.co.uk

Landlocked Brewery Handle Bar, 54a King Street, Alfreton, Derbyshire DE55 7DD | 07845 609585 landlockedbrewery.co.uk

Langton Brewery Grange Farm, Welham Rd, Thorpe Langton, Market Harborough, Leicestershire LE16 7TU 01858 540116 | langtonbrewery.co.uk

Leatherbritches Brewery Annwell Lane, Smisby, Ashby-de-la-Zouch, Leicestershire LE65 2TA 07976 279253 | leatherbritches.co.uk

Lincoln Green Brewing Company Unit E5 Enterprise Park, Wigwam Ln, Hucknall, Nottinghamshire NG15 7SZ | 01159 634233 lincolngreenbrewing.co.uk

Lincolnshire Brewing Company 15 Main Rd, Langworth, Lincoln, Lincolnshire LN3 5BJ 01522 595787 | lincolnshirebrewingco.co.uk

Linear Brewing Company Chaworth Road, Bingham, Nottinghamshire NG13 8EU linear.beer

Littleover Brewery 9, Robinsons Industrial Estate, Shaftesbury St, Derby, Derbyshire DE23 8NL | 01332 987100 | littleoverbrewery.co.uk

Magpie Brewery Unit 4, Ashling Court, Iremonger Road, Nottingham, Nottinghamshire NG2 3JA 01158 748467 | magpiebrewery.com

Market Bosworth Brewery Willow Farm Business Centre, Stoke Golding, Leicestershire CV13 6EU 01455 377855 | marketbosworthbrewery.co.uk

Matlock Wolds Farm Brewery South Barn, Cavendish Rd, Farm Ln, Matlock, Derbyshire DE4 3GZ 01629 697989 | woldsfarm.co.uk

Maypole Brewery North Laithes Farm, Wellow Road, Eakring, Nottinghamshire NG22 0AN 07971 277598 | maypolebrewery.co.uk

Milestone Brewery Great North Rd, Cromwell, Nottinghamshire NG23 6JE | 01636 822255 milestonebrewery.co.uk

Moody Fox Brewery The Hilcote Country Club, Hilcote Lane, Hilcote, Alfreton, Derbyshire DE55 5HR | 07702 253235

Mouselow Farm Brewery Mouselow Farm Cottage, Padfield, Glossop, Derbyshire SK13 7QQ 07920 048252

Muirhouse Brewery Unit 1, Enterprise Court, Manners Industrial Estate, Manners Road, Derbyshire DE7 8EW | 07916 590525 muirhousebrewery.co.uk

Navigation Brewery Trent Navigation Inn, 17 Meadow Ln, Nottingham, Nottinghamshire NG2 3HS 01159 869 877 | navigationbrewery.com

Neon Raptor Brewing Unit 14, Ave A, Sneinton Market, Nottingham, Nottinghamshire NG1 1DT 07367 358661 | neonraptorbrewingco.com

Newark Brewery 77, William Street, Newark on Trent, Nottinghamshire NG24 1QU | 07804 609917 newarkbrewery.co.uk

Newby Wyke Brewery Grantham, Lincolnshire NG31 9SN | 01476 565682 newbywyke.co.uk

Nottingham Brewery 17 St Peter's St, Nottingham, Nottinghamshire NG7 3EN
01159 422649 | nottinghambrewery.co.uk

Nutbrook Brewery 2 Belper Rd, Stanley Common, West Hallam, Derbyshire DE7 6FP | 0800 458 2460
nutbrookbrewery.com

Old Sawley Brewing Company The White Lion, 352a Tamworth Rd, Long Eaton, Nottingham, Nottinghamshire NG10 3AT
01158 370250 | oldsawley.com

Oldershaw Brewery 2, Barkston Heath, Barkston, Grantham, Lincolnshire NG32 2DE | 01476 572135
oldershawbrewery.com

Peak Ales The Barn Brewery, Chatsworth, Bakewell, Derbyshire DE45 1NH
01246 583737 | peakales.co.uk

Pentrich Brewing Co Unit B, Asher Lane, Ripley, Derbyshire DE5 3RE | 01773 741700
pentrichbrewing.co.uk

Pheasantry Brewery High Brecks Farm, Lincoln Rd, East Markham, Newark, Nottinghamshire NG22 0SN
01777 872728 | pheasantrybrewery.co.uk

Priors Well Brewery Old Mill Lane Industrial Estate, Mansfield Woodhouse, Mansfield, Nottinghamshire NG19 9BG | 01623 632393
priorswellbrewery.co.uk

Roebuck Brewery The Roebuck, Main Rd, Draycott in the Clay, Ashbourne, Derbyshire DE6 5BT
01283 821135 | theroebuckdraycott.co.uk

Shiny Brewing Old Hall Mill Business Park Alfreton Rd, 10, Little Eaton, Derbyshire DE21 5EJ
01332 902809 | shinybrewing.com

Shipstone's Brewery (The Fox & Crown)
Little Star Brewery, 33 Church St, Old Bashford, Nottingham, Nottinghamshire NG6 0GA
01158 374200 | shipstones.com

Springhead Brewery Main St, Laneham, Retford, Nottinghamshire DN22 0NA | 01777 229020
springhead.co.uk

The Bentley Brook Brewing Co Lumsdale Mill, Lumsdale, Matlock, Derbyshire DE4 5EX
07483 831640 | bentleybrook.co.uk

The Cat Asylum Brewing Co 12 Besthorpe Rd, Collingham, Newark, Nottinghamshire NG23 7NP
01636 892229 | cat-asylum.com

The Collyfobble Brewery Hackney Ln, Barlow, Dronfield, Derbyshire S18 7TD | 01145 539999
collyfobblebrewery.com

The Fuddy Duck Brewery Unit 12, Kirton Business Park, Willington Road, Boston, Lincolnshire PE20 1NN
07881 818875 | thefuddyduckbrewery.co.uk

The West End Brewery 68-70 Braunstone Gate, Leicester, Leicestershire LE3 5LG | 07875 745302
thewestendbrewery.co.uk

Thorley's Craft Beer 30 East Street, Ilkeston, Derbyshire DE7 5JB | 07899 067723
thorleyscraftbeer.co.uk

Thornbridge Brewery Riverside Brewery, Buxton Rd, Bakewell, Derbyshire DE45 1GS
01629 815999 | thornbridgebrewery.co.uk

Tom Herrick's Brewery The Stable House, Main Street, Carlton on Trent, Newark, Nottinghamshire NG23 6NW
07877 542331 | tomherricksbrewery.co.uk

Torrside Brewing The Wharf Warehouse, Hibbert St, New Mills, High Peak, Derbyshire SK22 3JJ
01663 745219 | torrside.co.uk

Totally Brewed 23 Chilwell Rd, Beeston, Nottingham, Nottinghamshire NG9 1EH
01159 984635 | totallybrewed.com

Townes Brewery 21 Lowgates, Staveley, Chesterfield, Derbyshire S43 3TT | 01246 472252

Urban Chicken Ale Heathfield Avenue, Ilkeston, Derbyshire | 07976 913395
urbanchickenale.co.uk

Welbeck Abbey Brewery Brewery Yard, Welbeck, Worksop, Nottinghamshire S80 3LT | 01909 512539
welbeckabbeybrewery.co.uk

West Midlands

Key

- #15 Attic Brew Co (P62)
- #16 Backyard Brewhouse (P64)
- #17 Banks's Brewery (P66)
- #18 Beat Brewery (P68)
- #19 Birmingham Brewing Company (P70)
- #20 Burning Soul (P72)
- #21 Byatt's Brewery (P74)
- #22 Dhillons Brewery (P76)
- #23 Enville Ales (P78)
- #24 Green Duck Beer Co. (P80)
- #25 Indian Brewery (P82)
- #26 RAN Ales (P84)
- #27 Sadler's Brewing Co. (P86)
- West Midlands breweries (P94)

#15 Attic Brew Co.

29B Mary Vale Road, Stirchley, Birmingham, West Midlands B30 2DA
atticbrewco.com | beer@atticbrewco.com | 07470 643758
@atticbrewco @atticbrewco @atticbrewco

About the brewery

One day someone will erect a statue in honour of the unknown home-brewer, such has been the influence of home-brewing on British craft beer. Sam and Oli, the guys who founded Attic, are two former home-brewers, starting out at university before stepping up production in the attic of Sam's Birmingham house (hence the brewery name). In 2018, Attic opened in a former factory space, which also acts as the brewery's popular and comfortable tap room (it's part of the Stirchley Beer Mile, see page 10).

It is here where beer-lovers can go at weekends and indulge themselves in Attic's tap list, which is a mixture of beer styles that are often neglected by British breweries (think Hefeweiss, Vienna Lager for starters) and more modern favourites. There are second hand sofas on which to lounge, a street food truck outside and children and dogs are welcome. 'Our tap room is an updated take on the traditional "local",' says Sam, 'acting as a meeting place for locals and travelling beer fans alike. We're committed to using beer to promote community and social interaction.' Investment in brewing equipment has also meant that Attic's beers can now be found in the on-trade, while there are plans for a barrel-ageing program and beers packaged in cans.

Signature brew

Long Weekend Wheat Beer, 5%
Damn good take on the Bavarian Hefeweiss style. Amber orange in colour, topped with a fine head of foam, brimming with banana custard and clove notes, refreshing and satisfying on the palate. Clean finish.

Established: 2018
Litres per year: 90,000

Brewery tours: Coming soon
Taphouse: Yes

Beers produced: 15
Open: Fri 4pm - 10pm, Sat 1pm - 10pm, Sun 2pm - 8pm

Established: 2008
Litres per year: 350,000
Brewery tours: No

Taphouse: Micro Pub, Heddin's Ford in Hednesford
Beers produced: 53

Open: Wed - Thurs 4pm - 10.30pm, Fri - Sat 12 - 10.30pm, Sun 12 - 7pm

#16 The Backyard Brewhouse

Gatehouse Trading Estate, Lichfield Rd, Brownhills, Walsall, West Midlands WS8 6JZ
tbb.uk.com | info@tbb.uk.com | 01543 360145
@backyardbrewhouse @backyardsnaps @backyardbeer

About the brewery

An award-winning Walsall-located brewery that began making beer in 2008, where English malted barley is used as the base for all their beers. Different combinations of hops, including varieties coming from the US, England, Slovenia and New Zealand, are utilised to produce a broad range of beers, both for the core range and monthly specials. Cask beer is very much at the centre of Backyard's operations, an ethos that sees their products distributed throughout the West Midlands and for sale in pubs in Birmingham, Wolverhampton and, naturally, their home town Walsall.

'We love ale and we brew it with the care and attention we believe it deserves,' says Brewery Director Mike Bates. 'We believe that creative brewing is all about not sticking to the same old formula. Since 2008 we have experimented with different combinations of hops and ingredients to find both traditional and excitingly new tasting ales.

'We've been in existence for just under 12 years now and grown steadily during this time, while maintaining a strong emphasis on quality and customer service. We have big plans for the next three to five years, with aims of growing our core business and moving into new areas of the trade, but at all times never losing focus of our key values.'

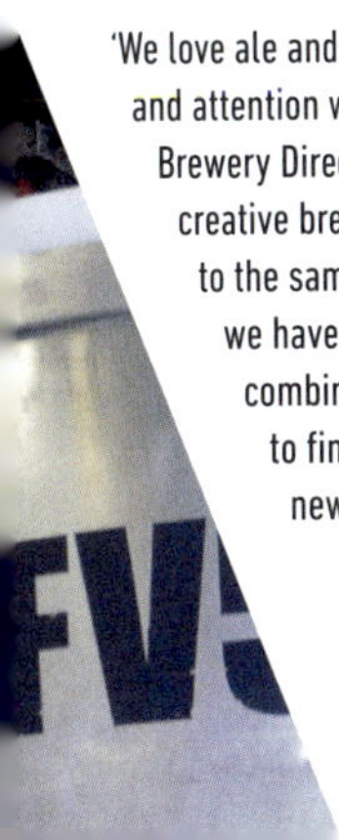

Signature brew

Blonde, 4.1%
Blonde-hued bitter with a citrus and pine nose and a dry, crip and hoppy palate. First produced in 2009, it now accounts for a third of the brewery's total sales.

#17 Banks's Brewery

Brewery Road, Chapel Ash, Wolverhampton, West Midlands WV1 4JT
bankssbeer.co.uk | bankssvisitorscentre@marstons.co.uk | 01902 329653
@bankssbeer @bankssbeer @bankssbeer

About the brewery

Banks's is an institution in the Black Country, a survivor from the Victorian days when mild was the drink of choice of the working man; it is a constant in the shifting scene of brewing, a survivor even, a thriver certainly as its history demonstrates. You won't go far in the Black Country, especially in its heartland of Wolverhampton where its beers have been brewed at the Park Brewery since 1875, without being able to savour beers such as its famous Amber Bitter as well as Sunbeam, which is the latest edition to the Banks's range, with its fresh zesty flavour proving to be a real hit with drinkers.

To get right into the heart of Banks's and understand its place in the Black Country, it does pay to book a brewery tour, where the whole brewing process is explained, the role of each ingredient examined and at the conclusion off you go to the brewery bar where Banks's beers can be sampled and contemplated. So go and try a pint of Banks's dark Mild, which as the brewers say, 'this is pure Black Country stuff. No one in the world can do it like us.'

Signature brew

Amber Bitter (3.8%)
Deep gold in colour, this has biscuity malt on the nose, which continues onto the palate alongside delicate citrus notes, before finishing bittersweet and with fruity overtones. Connoisseurs suggest it delightful with pork scratchings.

Established: 1875
Litres per year: 10,409028
Brewery tours: Yes
Taphouse: No

Beers produced: 4
Open: Tues - Wed 11am - 1:30pm, 2pm - 5pm,
Thurs & Fri 10am - 1:30am, 2pm - 6pm,
Sat 10am - 1:30pm, 2pm - 5pm.

Established: 2016
Litres per year: 50,000

Brewery tours: No
Taphouse: Yes
Beers produced: 9

Open:
Fri 2pm - 10pm,
Sat midday - 10pm

#18 Beat Brewery

Unit 9, Old Forge Trading Estate, Dudley Road, Lye, Stourbridge, West Midlands DY9 8EL
beatales.com | beer@beatales.com | 01384 469890
@beatalesbrewery @beatbrewery @BeatAlesBrewery

About the brewery

Beat actually started life in the small Somerset village of North Curry. In 2018 it was relocated up the M5 to Lye, which is close to Stourbridge. As beer names such as Funk, Raver and New Wave might suggest, there is a musical influence underpinning Beat's approach to brewing, or as the brewery says, 'we combine the mastery of craft beer with the artistry of some of the most influential music around to create our music inspired craft beers.

'We aim to give our customers the feel good factor from tasting the aromas and flavours that are produced from each individual beer. All of our beers are completely natural and suitable for vegans, because we do not use isinglass finings. Instead, we use a seaweed based fining meaning the process to clear the beer will happen, but just not as rapidly and they won't be crystal clear, rather as we like to say, "with a natural mystic haze'.

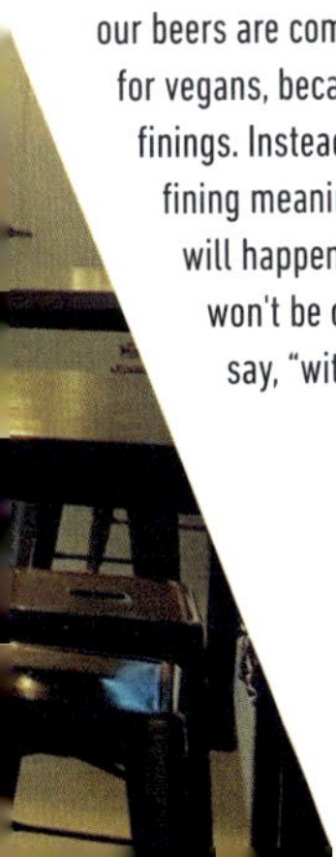

To get a feel for Beat's approach to rock'n'roll and beer, it pays to take the train to Lye and visit its recently opened tap room, which is next to the brewery. This is a showcase for its beers on cask, keg or in a bottle, and also gives drinkers the chance to try Beat's newest beers before they go into the trade.

Signature brew

Funk (5.5%)
Dry-hopped IPA that pulsates with the charge of New World hops, which give off tropical and citrus notes alongside a clean malt base. As the brewery says, 'guaranteed to get your groove on when the bassline drops'.

#19 Birmingham Brewing Company

Unit 17, Stirchley Trading Estate, Hazelwell Rd, Birmingham, West Midlands B30 2PF
birminghambrewingcompany.co.uk | info@birminghambrewingcompany.co.uk | 01217 240399
@Brumbrewery @Brumbrewery @Brumbrewery

About the brewery

Founded in 2016, the aim of Birmingham Brewing Company is to provide great tasting, high quality and locally brewed beer in a socially conscious manner.

With this in mind, Welsh mountain water, British floor-malted barley and hops from the most recent harvest are used in the brewing process, ensuring maximum flavour. Brummie Beers, such as Pale Brummie and Stout Brummie are vegan and gluten free, meaning they can be enjoyed by all.

As the first brewery in Stirchley, Birmingham Beer Company upholds social responsibility by maintaining environmentally friendly packaging and waste management, supporting local charities by donating goods, services and time, and offering local students internships with the aim of giving valuable work experience. Located on Stirchley Beer Mile (see page 10), the brewery hosts a tap room, tours and a beer school so regular visits can give drinkers an idea of the brewery's modus operandi.

When you visit, you might even notice a whirring canning machine. This new addition to the brewery maximizes efficiency, taste and freshness and also helps with recycling. Birmingham Brewing Company knows the journey it is taking and beer-lovers would be well-advised to join in.

Signature brew

Confused Brummie, 6%
The style is white stout and it looks like a pale ale but tastes like a stout with roasty flavours and earthy English hop character. Once you get over the confusion, this is a complex and masterful beer.

Established: 2016
Litres per year: 80,000
Brewery tours: Yes
Taphouse: Yes
Beers produced: 30
Open: Fri 4pm - 10pm & Sat midday - 10pm

Established: 2019
Litres per year: 46,800

Brewery tours: Yes
Taphouse: Yes
Beers produced: 135

Open: Friday 4pm - 8pm, Sat 1pm - 8pm

#20 Burning Soul

51 Mott Street, Birmingham, West Midlands B19 3HE
burningsoulbrewing.com | burningsoulbrew@gmail.com | 01214 391490
@burningsoulbrewery @burningsoulbrewery @burningsoulbrew

About the brewery

Two friends, Rich Murphy and Chris Small, spent several years discussing beer and home-brewing it. Eventually, they came to a decision, it was time to set up their own brewery, which they did in 2016, in the former home of Two Towers Brewery, who had moved to larger premises.

The name of the brewery came from Murphy and Small's burning passion for making beer and their aim was 'to constantly brew new beers and try new methods and ingredients to develop our beers and ourselves as brewers'. In 2017, six months into brewing commercially, Burning Soul was voted best new brewery in the West Midlands by members of the RateBeer community and things have continued to improve.

To understand and appreciate the ethos of Burning Soul, make your way to the tap room, which is described as the 'heart and soul' of the brewery. It is here where the brewers can get first hand feedback from drinkers on their latest brews. There are always 12-14 of Burning Soul's beers on draft, which are only sold in halves or thirds so as to encourage people to try new beers. Saturday afternoons also see regular brewery tours, which include taster beers.

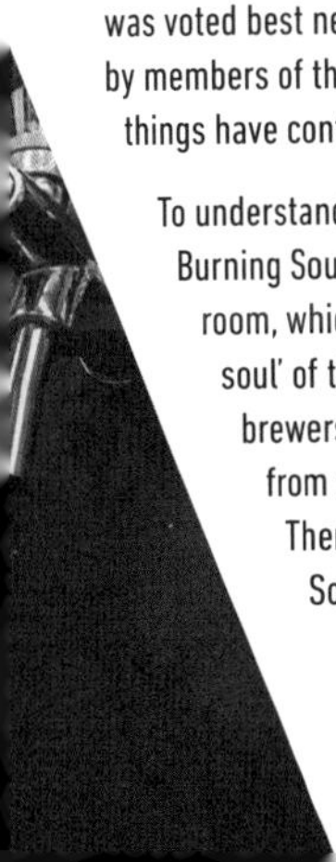

Signature brew

Coconut Porter, 7%
This is a robust porter which has toasted coconut added to the mix – this results in a dark beer with hints of chocolate and the smoothness of the coconut. It is also one of Burning Soul's oldest recipes going back to the home-brew days of six years ago.

#21 Byatt's Brewery

Units 7 & 8, Lythalls Lane Industrial Estate, Lythalls Lane, Coventry, West Midlands CV6 6FL
byattsbrewery.co.uk | info@byattsbrewery.co.uk | 02476 637996
@Byatts-Brewery @Byatts-Brewery @ByattsBrewery

About the brewery

Located in Coventry and opened in 2011, Byatt's was the first commercially successful brewery in the city for 80 years. Founder and brewer is Lee Byatt, who also comes from Coventry and whose declared aim is 'to produce great tasting, quality beer to pubs and clubs within the region. We want to be the brewer of choice where publicans have the freedom to use us'.

Byatt's beers are very much a celebration of Coventry with six of them having a connection through their names: XK Dark, a classic mild, pays gratitude to the city for its effort in the war; Coventry Bitter was the first beer brewed; Big Cat celebrates the car industry within Coventry; Phoenix Gold the old and new cathedrals rising from the ashes; Urban Red commemorates that historically Coventry had a thriving textile industry and Regal Blonde remembers Lady Godiva.

The brewery also has a lively tap house on site, which is open Thursday-Saturdays (check website for times), while regular tours and tastings enable lovers of Byatt's to see the process and also engage in a tutored tasting. When he opened the brewery one of Lee Byatt's intentions was to make it part of the city – it certainly seems as if he has succeeded.

Signature brew

Phoenix Gold, 4.2%
This is a golden ale which marries an initial malt sweetness with a crisp, fresh hop flavour and a rounded bitter finish. It is the brewery's best selling beer.

Established: 2011
Litres per year: 100,000

Brewery tours: Yes, and beer tasting events
Taphouse: Yes

Beers produced: 37
Open: Thurs 4pm - 9pm, Fri 4 - 9pm, Sat 12 - 9pm

Established: 2015
Litres per year: 100,000

Brewery tours: Yes
Taphouse: Yes
Beers produced: 20

Open: Fri 5pm - midnight (Open for all Wasps and Coventry City FC home games)

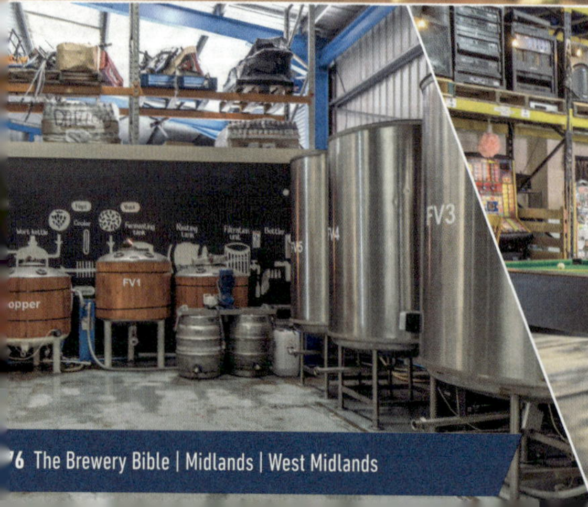

#22 Dhillon's

Unit 14a, Hales Industrial Estate, Rowleys Green Lane, Coventry, West Midlands CV6 6AL
dhillonsbrewery.com | info@dhillonsbrewery.com | 02476 667413
@Dhillonsbrewery @Dhillonsbrewery @Dhillonsbrewery

About the brewery

Coventry is home for Dhillon's who started brewing in 2015. 'Our mission is to put the Midlands on the brewery map one beer at a time,' says founder Dal Dhillon. 'We aim to brew beer that we enjoy and we hope to make the beer-lover as passionate about beer as we are. We are striving to make a brand and brew beer that all people can enjoy.'

The brewery also has a lively tap room, a warehouse-style space with murals on the wall – it is usually open every Friday evening, but due to its closeness to the Ricoh stadium, pints will also be pulled during Coventry FC and Wasps match-days. Or as Dhillon says, 'we have a tipplers' fortress where our range of ales get the sip of approval from our eager guinea pigs who are more than happy to put themselves forward'.

The tipplers' fortress, or tap room, is the place where Dhillon's beers, both on cask and in bottle, can be sampled and evaluated, while their beers are also widely available in the free trade in Coventry and further afield. It does seem as if the brewery's approach to making beer that they and others enjoy seems to work, as plenty of awards have come Dhillon's way including a SIBA National Bronze medal for Red Rebel IPA and, more recently, a Gold from the World Beer Awards for the speciality steam lager, The Alegre.

Signature brew

Red Rebel IPA (6.2%)
Award-winning India Red Ale that uses both European and American hops to produce a well-hopped beer with plenty of flavour and a bittersweet finish.

#23 Enville Brewery

Hollies Lane, Cox Green, Enville, Nr. Stourbridge DY7 5LG
envilleales.com | info@envilleales.com | 01384 873728
@envillebrewery @envillebrewery @envillebrewery

About the brewery

1993 saw the foundation of the brewery in a set of unused stables on a farm in the village of Enville, an idyllic location which is surrounded by the beautiful rolling hills and valleys of South Staffordshire. Almost immediately Enville made an impact with Enville Ale, which was based on a 19th century recipe that used honey; at the time there were not many honey beers on the market and Enville's won many friends on the beer scene with it. Ale has remained a popular choice, but is also joined by Ginger, White and Old Porter amongst the core range and during the colder months regular sightings can be had of Gothic Stout and their winter warmer Blizzard.

Given its rural setting, it comes as no surprise to discover that Enville takes it water from a natural well, while it has an eco-friendly waste reed bed filtration system. Their beers are available at over 100 pubs and clubs throughout the Midlands and feature regularly at beer festivals nationwide. 'Our team may be small, but our passion for creating and serving high quality ales is huge. 2018 brought new members to the team, and we are so excited to be part of Enville's next chapter.'

Signature brew

Enville Ale, 4.5%
Based on a 19th century recipe from the great-great aunt of Enville's original founder, this traditional 'beekeeper's ale' is light in colour with fruity notes and a hint of honey sweetness, which acts as a foil to the dry hoppy taste.

Established: 1993
Litres per year: 630,000

Brewery tours: Coming soon
Taphouse: No

Beers produced: 8
Open: Mon - Thurs 9am - 4pm, Fri 9am - 3pm

Established: 2013
Litres per year: 200,000

Brewery tours: Yes
Taphouse: Yes
Beers produced: 50

Open: Fri 4 - 11pm & Sat 1 - 7pm

#24 Green Duck Beer Co.

Unit 13 Gainsborough Estate, Rufford Road, West Midlands DY9 7ND
greenduckbrewery.co.uk | beer@greenduckbrewery.co.uk | 01384 377666
@GreenDuckBeerCo @green_duck_brewery @greenduckbrew

About the brewery

If you want to discover what makes Green Duck so popular then get a train to Stourbridge and take a few minutes walk to get to the brewery bar, which is open every weekend. Here, behind a glass partition, you will see the gleaming, stainless steel brewing kit where regular cask beers such as Duck & Cover and Sitting Duck can be enjoyed, in the company of seasonal specials such as Uprising and Supremacy.

Situated in a large, light and airy warehouse space, Green Duck also hosts beer festivals and a gin festival through the year, and over the period the bar has been open it has become a true community hub which welcomes families as much as those in search of ticking off Green Duck's beers. The majority of the brewery's beers go into cask, with the rest in keg and can with the brewery's self-declared aim being to 'produce hop forward beers that are approachable and easy to drink'.

Green Duck beers are also widely available throughout the West Midlands and further afield through its distribution partners.

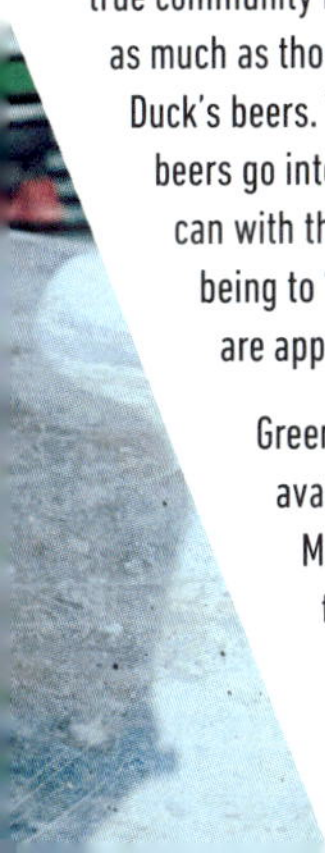

However, mark a note in your diary for Friday or Saturday's train to Stourbridge and discover the essence of Green Duck.

Signature brew

Duck & Cover, 4%
Session IPA where the hops Simcoe and Mosaic really shine through. One of the brewery's core beers and its best seller. The brewery says that this is the kind of beer that you can just sit there and drink it all day.

#25 The Indian Brewery

Unit 5, Aston Expressway Industrial Estate, Birmingham, West Midlands B6 4EX
indianbrewery.com | drink@indianbrewery.com | 01212 969000
@indianbrewery @indianbrewery @indianbrewery

About the brewery

Founded in 2014, The Indian Brewery produces a sparkling range of craft beers, including Birmingham Lager, a traditional well-hopped IPA and Bombay Honey, which as the name suggests has honey added to the mix. These are all beers that have gone down well with Birmingham beer-lovers and can be found in a well-selected series of outlets.

'We brew some awesome craft beers whilst maintaining quality of colour, aroma and taste,' says founder Jaspal Purewal. 'We value innovation in both our craft and design and carry a strong appreciation for the boundless limits created by hard work. We're Influenced by the natural elements of our everyday living, fuelled by creative thinking and powered to develop high quality beers.'

Initially a stand-alone brewery, you can get a full flavour (in the true sense of the meaning) of The Indian Brewery by visiting its modern and dynamically styled brace of tap rooms, one in the Jewellery Quarter in Birmingham, the other in Solihull, where innovative and delicious Indian street food is served alongside the brewery's beers.

There is more to come from The Indian Brewery though as Purewal explains: 'We are currently installing our brand new brew-kit at our new premises, which will be open to the public very soon with an onsite tap room.'

Signature brew

Birmingham Lager, 4.5%
Created by the brewery with the aim of representing the soul and sensibility of Birmingham, this is an unfiltered Pilsner-style lager that bursts with refreshing citrus and floral aromas and has a clean and buoyant flavour.

Established: 1993
Litres per year: 630,000

Brewery tours: Coming soon
Taphouse: No

Beers produced: 8
Open: Mon - Thurs 9am - 4pm, Fri 9am - 3pm

Established: 2014
Litres per year: 200,000

Brewery tours: Yes
Taphouse: Yes
Beers produced: 14

Open: Thurs 5pm - 8pm, Fri - Sat 12pm - late, 2nd Sun of the month

#26 RAN Ales

Unit 8, Imex Business Park, Ormonde Street, Fenton, Stoke-on-Trent, West Midlands ST4 3NP
ranales.co.uk | sales@ranales.co.uk | 07843 092620
@LtdRan @LtdRan @LtdRan

About the brewery

It was July 2014 and Neville Smith was celebrating his 53rd birthday in a local pub, The Bench and Bar in his home town of Fenton, just outside Stoke. He took in a barrel of beer with him and the regulars loved it. This was the first RAN Ales brew and Smith hasn't looked back. Since then he has created an enviable portfolio of craft ales that range from light and hoppy pale ales through to malty bitters and stouts with names such as Rum & Raisin Stout and Cherry Chilli Stout.

'I am always creating new brews,' he says, 'and never know what I am going to make next! All new brews are tested on the bar of our Real Ale Bar, which is at the brewery, with our customers and we sometimes use their feedback to create the names of the beers. The latest is a wheat beer called 'Ranhalla' in honour of the Viking wedding event we hosted in the bar.

'Our regulars can enjoy the sun at our bar in the summer and our log fire in the winter. Most of our customers have discovered us by recommendation from others and we are always welcoming new people into the bar each week. We have fun, we laugh, and we enjoy what we do and people tell us it shows. We are very proud of what we have created and feel very lucky to be doing something we love.'

Signature brew

Hedgehopper, 4%
A light gold bitter with a delicate fruitiness on the nose and palate and which is a livelier and lighter ale than some of the others in Ran Ales' range. 'Hedge Hopping' was a popular dare or 'Doffa' in Stoke slang which involved jumping over each hedge from house to house without getting caught by the neighbours.

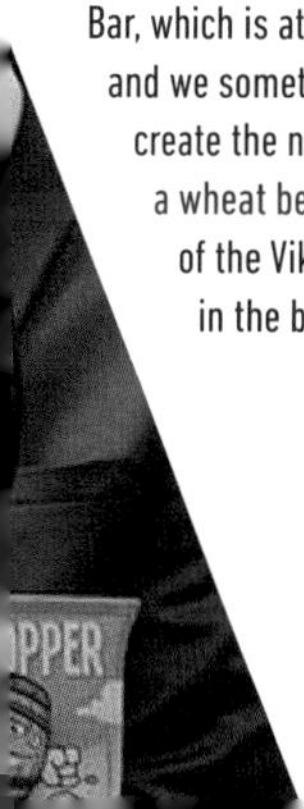

#27 Sadler's Brewing Co.

Station House, Station Drive, Lye, Stourbridge, West Midlands DY9 8ER
sadlersales.co.uk | beer@sadlersales.co.uk | 01384 895230
@sadlersbrewco @sadlersbrewco @sadlersbrewco

About the brewery

The original Sadler's Brewery was founded in 1861 and continued until 1927, but in 2004 descendants of the former owners began brewing again and it remains very much a thriving family-run craft brewery that supplies its beers to bars, restaurants and shops throughout the region and beyond. 'Quality and passion are at the heart of everything we do,' says Chris Sadler, the brewery's Managing Director. 'Our highly experienced team produces truly hand-crafted beer and spirits that continue to win the hearts of our loyal customers throughout the country and indeed the world.'

Sadler's success has helped them to expand extensively so as to be able to cope with increased demand for their beers. There are a couple of different sized breweries on the Lye site, with experimentation enabled by the five-barrel kit, while the 60-barrel one allows larger volume production of the beers, of which a wide variety are produced in cask, keg, bottle and can. These include the popular Peaky Blinder range, which acts as a historical link with the original Sadler's, a business that ran pubs in and around Birmingham and the Black Country and which members of the Peaky Blinders probably frequented.

Signature brew

Peaky Blinder Pale Ale, 4.3%
Award-winning light-coloured and refreshing pale ale that makes use of English hops and barley. Fruity nose with a gentle fruitiness and bitterness on the palate that leads to an uplifting citrusy finish.

Established: 1861
Litres per year: 4,000,000

Brewery tours: Yes
Taphouse: Yes
Beers produced: 17

Open: Brewhouse Weds - Sat 12pm - midnight

#28 Brewhouse & Kitchen Lichfield

1 Bird Street, Lichfield, West Midlands WS13 6PW
brewhouseandkitchen.com/lichfield | lichfield@brewhouseandkitchen.com | 01543 224740
@BKLich @bk_lichfield @bklichfield

About the venue

You can sit in the modernist surroundings of Lichfield's Brewhouse & Kitchen and catch some brewing theatre as the brewers go about their business, mashing in, adding hops and keeping an eye on the fermentation.

Obviously with one of their beers to hand, such as the hazy and citrusy Spellman Sam Tropical IPA or one of their Guest's Choice beers, a small batch range of beers voted for by the public. The venue also offers brewery experience days, beer masterclasses and there is a meet the brewer event every Thursday night.

Mission statement

We are a microbrewery and pub offering delicious brews brewed in-house and equally scrumptious dishes from our kitchen, which we match with the beers and we also cook with our beers! Everyone is welcome at Brewhouse & Kitchen, including well behaved children, dogs and adults. Let us know if you happen to be celebrating a special event or birthday... don't be shy, we'd love to celebrate with you!

Open:
11am - 11pm
Established: 2017

No. of beers sold:
10
Takeout: Yes

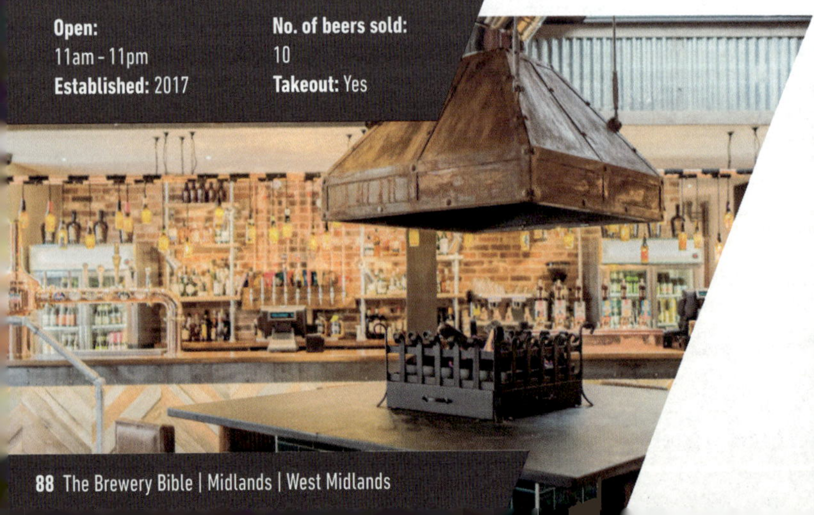

Open:
Mon - Thurs
11am - 11pm,
Fri - Sat 11am - 1am,
Sun 11am - 10.30pm

Established: 2017

No. of beers sold: 70

Takeout: Yes

#29 Brewhouse & Kitchen Nottingham

Trent Bridge, Nottingham, Nottinghamshire NG2 2GS
brewhouseandkitchen.com/nottingham | nottingham@brewhouseandkitchen.com | 01159 867960
@BKNottingham @bk_nottingham @BKNottingham1

About the venue

Standing on the Trent Bridge, this popular brewpub and restaurant was built in the late 1860s when it was then called the Town Arms. Over the decades, it had several names and its current incarnation dates from 2017, when gleaming brewing equipment and a vibrant attitude towards beer and food was introduced.

Meet the brewer events are weekly and attendees are actively encouraged to ask questions, while beer and food matching, beer masterclasses and brewery experience days also take place.

Mission statement

We're a bit different from your traditional pub – we brew our own, unique craft beers on-site in our brew-tiful microbrewery. As well as matching every dish on our menu to a style of beer we also love cooking with beer – so be sure to keep an eye out for recipes that make use of the beers we brew, right next to where you enjoy them. We want people to love beer – we want you to sample our beers and find your favourite – just ask and we can talk you through them.

#30 KILDER

5 Shaw's Passage, Digbeth, Birmingham, West Midlands B5 5JG
kilderbar.co.uk | info@originalpattymen.com | 01216 432546
@kilderbar @kilder_bar @kilder_bar

About the venue

Before KILDER opened in 2018, there was the Original Patty Men restaurant in a railway arch beneath Moor Street station. Then owners Tom Maher and Scott O'Byrne set up a bar in the arch next door, a light and airy space with a Scandi feel to the decor and a momentous list of craft beer including local heroes such as GlassHouse Beer and Burning Soul, alongside succulent grilled cheese sandwiches. Plenty of tap takeovers have occurred with breweries such as Siren, North, Mikkeller, Amundsen and Lervig as well as food and beer pairing nights which take place regularly - check the site for updated information.

Mission statement

We want to share our passion for craft beer, cider and natural wine by continually rotating our offerings and always looking for unique and interesting products from breweries and vineyards around the world. We are based in the railway arches under Moor Street station which gives us a unique environment to sell our beer from and we have tried our very best to make use of such an interesting space and create a relaxed and friendly environment.

Open: Wed 5pm - 11pm,
Thur - Sat 12pm - 11pm,
Sun 12pm - 9pm
Established: 2018

No. of beers sold:
15 changing taps &
50 cans/bottles
Takeout: Yes

Open:
Mon - Thurs
11am - 11pm,
Fri - Sat
11am - midnight,
Sun 11am - 8pm
Established: 2015
No. of beers sold:
8 cask, 16 craft
Takeout: Yes

#31 Purecraft Bar & Kitchen

30 Waterloo Street, Birmingham, West Midlands B2 5TJ
purecraftbars.com | info@purecraftbars.com | 01212 375666
@purecraftbars @purecraftbarandkitchen @purecraftbars

About the venue

Come to Purecraft to evaluate the beers of Purity as well as other craft beers from across the country and indeed the world. This is Purity's urban hub, a contrast to its gentle rural heartland where the beers are brewed. Things to do apart from drink? The UBrew Beer Club is a popular event where Purity's brew team provide advice and brewing tips to home-brewers, while dishes on the menu offer up beer-matching suggestions. Oh, and don't forget Purecraft's award-winning Scotch eggs.

Mission statement

We match crafted beer, real food and top people to create a great experience in the middle of Birmingham city centre! We opened in 2014 and a year later won the Great British Pub Awards National Award for Best Beer Pub. We also host tap takeovers, invite home-brewers in for the UBrew Beer Club, launch new Purity beers and generally aim to give people a great and unforgettable time.

#32 The Wildcat Tap

1381-1383 Pershore Road, Stirchley, Birmingham, West Midlands B30 2JR
stirchleywildcat.co.uk | info@stirchleywildcat.co.uk
@wildcatB30 @wildcatB30

About the venue

2015 saw the opening of the Wildcat Tap at a different premises from where it now calls home. Then in 2019 it moved into an empty and much bigger unit that used to be a restaurant and is now a clean and modern interior that looks onto Pershore Road. Since then, it's become one of the essential stop-overs on the Stirchley Beer Mile as well as for locals who appreciate its selection of beers, which come from brewers such as Fixed Wheel, Twisted Barrel, Burning Soul, and their near neighbours GlassHouse Beer.

Mission statement

First and foremost, we aim to be a friendly neighbourhood bar. We are also dedicated to putting on an interesting, ever changing line-up of beers in both cask and keg, which are all cold-stored at serving temperature for optimum enjoyment. All draught beers are available to take away in 750ml glass bottles.

Open:
Mon - Fri, 5pm - 11pm,
Sat, 2pm - 11pm,
Sun, 2pm - 6pm

Established: 2019
No. of beers sold:
Up to 8 keg & 2-4 cask
Takeout: Yes

THE BEST IN BEER,
FROM THE GREATEST BREWERIES,
DELIVERED TO YOUR DOOR.
Over 600 beers in bottles and cans. The best in home draught with THE SUB.
Stories and insights from the brewers. All online and delivered in a box.
HONEY DEW
RED MY LIPS
FRAGILE
BREEKBAAR
ZERBRECHLICH
BEERWULF
JAIPUR
Tiny Rebel
Enjoy responsibly.
BEERWULF.COM

West Midlands Breweries

AJ's Ales 12 Long Acre St, Walsall, West Midlands WS2 8QG | 07860 585911 | ajsales.com

Attic Brew Co Unit 29b, Mary Vale Industrial Estate, Stirchley, Birmingham, West Midlands B30 2DA | 07967 592448 | atticbrewco.com

Bank's Brewery (Marstons) Brewery Road, Wolverhampton, West Midlands WV1 4JT 01902 329653 | bankssbeer.co.uk

Batham's Brewery 10 Delph Rd, Brierley Hill, West Midlands DY5 2TN | 01384 77229 bathams.co.uk

Beat Ales 9, Old Forge Trading Estate, Dudley Rd, Stourbridge, West Midlands DY9 8EL 01823 479299 | beatales.com

Beowulf Brewing Co Pool Rd, Burntwood, Walsall, West Midlands WS8 7NL | 01543 454067 beowulfbrewery.com

Birmingham Brewing Co Unit 15, Stirchley Trading Estate, Hazelwell Rd, Birmingham, West Midlands B30 2PF | 01217 240399 birminghambrewingcompany.co.uk

Blackcountry Ales Brewery 69 Third Avenue, Pensnett Trading Estate, Kingswinford, West Midlands DY6 7FD | 01384 401820 blackcountryales.co.uk

Burning Soul Brewing 1, 51 Mott St, Birmingham, West Midlands B19 3HE 01214 391490 | burningsoulbrewing.com

Byatt's Brewery Lythalls Lane Industrial Estate, 7-8, Coventry, West Midlands CV6 6FL 02476 637996 | byattsbrewery.co.uk

Craddocks Brewery (Duke William Pub) 25 Coventry Street, Stourbridge, West Midlands DY8 1EP | 01384 397218 craddocksbrewery.com

Davenports Brewery 11 New St, Birmingham, Smethwick, West Midlands B66 2AJ 01215 554867 | davenports.co.uk

Dig Brew Co 43 River St, Birmingham, West Midlands B5 5SA 01217 732111 | digbrewco.com

Dhillons Brewery Unit 14a, Hales Industrial Estate, Rowley's Green Ln, Coventry, Warwickshire CV6 6AT | 02476 667413 dhillonsbrewery.com

Enville Ales Hollies Ln, Cox Green, Stourbridge, West Midlands DY7 5LG 01384 873728 | envilleales.com

Fixed Wheel Brewery 9 Long Lane Trading Estate, Long Lane, Blackheath, Halesowen, West Midlands B62 9LD | 07766 162794 fixedwheelbrewery.co.uk

Fownes Brewing Company (The Jolly Crispin) 25 Clarence Street, Dudley, West Midlands DY3 1UL 07790 766844 | fownesbrewing.co.uk

GlassHouse Beer Unit 6b, Waterside Business Park, 1649-1652, Pershore Rd, Birmingham, West Midlands B30 3DR | 07956 774142 facebook.com/glasshousebeerco

Green Duck Brewery Gainsborough Trading Estate, Rufford Rd, Stourbridge, West Midlands DY9 7ND | 01384 377666 greenduckbrewery.co.uk

Holden's Brewery George St, Woodsetton, Dudley, West Midlands DY1 4LW
01902 880051 | holdensbrewery.co.uk

Kinver Brewery Unit 1, Britch Farm, Rocky Wall, Compton DY7 5NW | 07715 842679
kinverbrewery.co.uk

Moseley Beer Co Unit 36, 14-20 George St, Birmingham, West Midlands B12 9RG
07507 209220 | moseleybeercompany.co.uk

New Invention Brewery Unit 2, Pinfold Industrial Estate, Walsall, West Midlands WS3 3JS
newinventionbrewery.co.uk

Newbridge Brewery Unit 3, Tudor House, Moseley Road, Bilston, West Midlands WV14 6JD
07970 456052 | newbridgebrewery.co.uk

Punchline Brewery 13 Monmore Road, Wolverhampton, West Midlands WV1 2TZ
01902 213063 | punchlinebrewery.co.uk

RAN Ales Unit 8, Ormonde St, Fenton, Stoke-on-Trent, West Midlands ST4 3RR
07843 092620 | ranales.co.uk

Red Moon Brewery Kimberley Avenue, Birmingham, West Midlands B8 3LB
redmoonbrewery.co.uk

Sadler's Brewing Co. Unit 2, Conyers Trading Estate, Station Drive, Stourbridge, West Midlands DY9 8ER | 01384 895230
sadlersales.co.uk

Sarah Hughes Brewery (The Beacon Hotel)
129 Bilston St, Dudley, West Midlands DY3 1JE
01902 883380 | sarahhughesbrewery.co.uk

Silhill Brewery Unit 1, Oak Farm, Hampton Ln, Catherine-de-Barnes, Hampton in Arden, Solihull, West Midlands B92 0JB
07977 444564 | silhillbrewery.co.uk

The Backyard Brewhouse Gatehouse Trading Estate, Lichfield Rd, Brownhills, Walsall, West Midlands WS8 6JZ | 01543 360145
thebackyardbrewhouse.com

The Indian Brewery Co Unit 5, Aston Express Way Industrial Estate, Pritchett Street, Birmingham, West Midlands B6 4EX
01212 969000 | indianbrewery.com

Toll End Brewery (Waggon & Horses)
131 Toll End Rd, Tipton, West Midlands DY4 0ET
01215 026453

Twisted Barrel Brewery Unit 11, FarGo Village, Far Gosford St, Coventry, Warwickshire CV1 5ED
02476 101701 | twistedbarrelale.co.uk

Two Towers Brewery 29 Shadwell St, Birmingham, West Midlands B4 6HG
01214 393738 | twotowersbrewery.co.uk

Warwickshire & Northamptonshire

#35
#34
#33
#36
#37
Key
#33 Great Oakley Brewery (P98)
#34 Maule Brewing Co. (P100)
#35 Purity Brewing Co (P102)
#36 Towcester Mill Brewery (P104)
#37 XT Brewing Company (P106)
Warwickshire &
Northamptonshire breweries (P112)

#33 Great Oakley Brewery

Ark Farm, High Street South, Tiffield, Northamptonshire NN12 8AB
greatoakleybrewery.co.uk | sales@greatoakleybrewery.co.uk | 01327 351759
@greatoakleybrewery greatoakleybrewery

About the brewery

Great Oakley was set up in the Northants village of the same name in 2005 by home-brewer and CAMRA activist Phil Greenway along with businessman Mike Evans, who handily happened to have some stables in which the brewery was located. Evans left to run a pub in 2007, and Greenway brought in the then 20-year-old Guy Jenkins as his apprentice. Great Oakley's beers proved to be spectacularly popular and in 2012 needing more space, it moved to its current location in the village of Tiffield and Guy now runs the operation solo.

According to owner Jenkins, 'we strive to make traditional, interesting, no-compromise beer to the highest standard possible'. Given the amount of awards the brewery has won (over 50 at both regions and national level from both SIBA and CAMRA), the brewery is more than living up to his statement of belief. Ten beers are regularly produced, which are served from cask and packaged in bottle, while special event beers are also created. The beers' names are a celebration of local landmarks such as the best bitter Harpers, whose name comes from Harpers Brook, a tributary of the River Nene which flows behind the original brewery, so you get a real sense of Northamptonshire place when drinking Great Oakley's beers.

Signature brew

Tiffield Thunderbolt, 4.2%
Pale and refreshing session IPA that uses two different hops from New Zealand; fruity, bittersweet with a dry and crisp finish.

Established: 2005
Litres per year: 85,000
Brewery tours: No
Taphouse: No
Beers produced: 10
Open: Mon - Fri 7am - 3pm

Established: 2014
Litres per year: Batch brew 1800 litres a time to demand

Brewery tours: Coming soon
Taphouse: Yes, Maule Collective, Northampton

Beers produced: 10
Open: Tue - Thurs midday - 10.30pm, Fri - Sat 12pm - 1am, Sun 12 - 7pm

#34 Maule Brewing Co.

4 Derngate, Northampton, Northamptonshire NN1 1UB
maulebrewing.com | hello@maulebrewing.com
@MauleBrewingCompany @maulebrewingco @MauleBrewingCo

About the brewery

Northampton is home for family business Maule Brewing Co., which began brewing in 2014 and whose credo is: 'Our mission is simple. Keep our beers simple and uncomplicated and produce beers that will stand the test of time. To focus on quality and consistency. This culminates in a small range of beers that stay true to style but are no means lacking in flavour and drinkability. We brew beers that we want to drink and hope the quality keeps people coming back for more! We just do our own thing and let other people do theirs.'

Its first beer was Lucky IPA, which won 'best of show' at Craft Beer Rising in 2016, though Maule also has a love for lagering, which was demonstrated by the second beer they released in 2014, an amber lager. This has been followed by a few since, including Mandarina Lager and Rocking Rakau NZ Pilsner. 'With our lagers we focus on the ingredients and the full cold conditioning period, which we think takes lager to another level. All of our beers are unfiltered and unfined. We continue to champion this style and it will always be at the forefront of what we do and not just an afterthought.'

In order to fully appreciate the approach of Maule, visit the Maule Collective, a tap room and bar in Northampton where their fresh beers, which are only brewed a mile away, as well as some of their favourite guest beers, can be enjoyed.

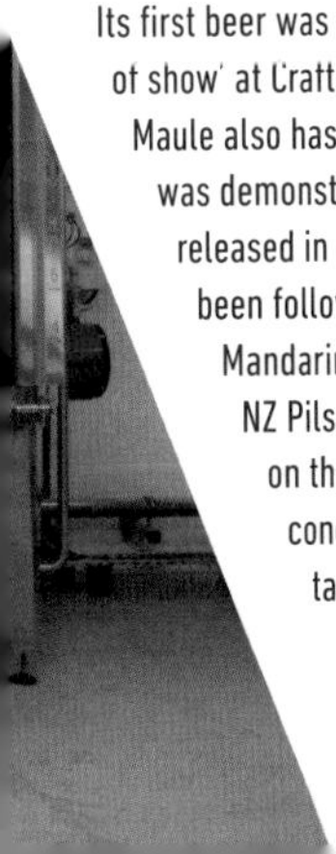

Signature brew

Lucky IPA, 5.5%
This fuses the vibrant hop varieties Galaxy, Mosaic and Simcoe, giving a rich peach and orange aroma, followed by a sweet caramel malt body with a clean mid palate bitterness that drifts away into a smooth finish.

#35 Purity Brewing Co

The Brewery, Upper Spernall Farm, Spernal Ln, Great Alne, Alcester, Warwickshire B49 6JF
puritybrewing.com | sales@puritybrewing.com | 01789 488007
@puritybrewingco @purityale @Purityale

About the brewery

Purity is an apt name for one of the Midlands' most popular breweries, given its commitment to supporting the environment and creating a sustainable business model (see page 16 for more on this). The brewing process only uses natural ingredients, recycling programmes are supported, while its waste products are recycled through a pond and wetland system, which helps to minimise carbon dioxide emissions and encourage wildlife diversity.

The brewery was set up in 2005 by Paul Halsey and James Minkin and the following year Frenchman Flo Vialan joined as head brewer, helping to create and maintain award-winning beers such as Pure UBU (named after a dog that once lived on the farm the brewery is based), Pure Gold and Longhorn IPA. Seven regular beers are produced in both cask and keg form, while there is also a growing appetite for their vegan-friendly, speciality keg range which includes Pure Helles, Session IPA (both also gluten-free) and Kveik IPA.

To get right into the heart of Purity, there are regular Saturday afternoon tours of the brewery where visitors can see the gleaming stainless steel vessels and hear about the brewing process, followed by that all important tasting in a cosy tap room. The brewery is also located in beautiful Warwickshire countryside so that's an extra bonus. And if you cannot wait until the weekend, there is an onsite shop where Purity's beers can be bought.

Signature brew

Pure UBU, 4.5%
Full-flavoured best bitter that is brewed with Maris Otter, crystal, black and wheat malts, with Pilgrim and Cascade hops added, all of which combine to give dark fruit notes and a bittersweet finish.

Established: 2005
Litres per year: 450,0000

Brewery tours: Yes
Taphouse: Yes
Beers produced: 10

Open: Mon - Fri 9am - 5pm, Sat 10am - 1pm

Established: 2014
Litres per year: 300,000
Brewery tours: Yes
Taphouse: Yes
Beers produced: 15
Open: Mon 5 - 8pm, Tues - Thurs 5 - 10.30pm, Fri 2 - 11pm, Sat 12 - 11pm & Sun 12 - 8pm

#36 Towcester Mill Brewery

Chantry Lane, Towcester, Northamptonshire NN12 6YY
towcestermillbrewery.co.uk | info@towcestermillbrewery.co.uk | 01327 437060
@Towcestermillbrewery @towcestermillbrewery @TowcesterMill

About the brewery

Home for Towcester Mill Brewery is a historic old mill that dates back to 1794 and which is Grade II listed. Within its beautiful interiors the five-barrel brewing kit produces a popular and award-winning selection of beers, both regulars such as Mill Race and Bell Ringer and seasonals and one-off beers like the mild Maius and the Christmas special Santa's Tipple.

The building is also on the local beer tourist trail as it boasts a tap room, with occasional live comedy and music nights; if the weather is favourable drinkers can relax in the large beer garden, which has views over Towcester water meadows and the beautiful Easton Neston estate.

The brewery also has a thriving annual membership scheme where members benefit from discounts as well as tours, exclusive members' evenings and beer launches. There is a real sense of a community about Towcester Mill Brewery with all its activities, while many of its beer names celebrate the surrounding countryside and the history of the area.

The 5.2% American Style IPA Roman Road refers to Watling Street, which passes nearby, and Saxon Shield, a recent SIBA award-winner, recalls Towcester's role in Anglo-Saxon times as part of the frontier between the kingdom of Wessex and the Danelaw.

Signature brew

Mill Race, 3.9%
Pale blonde in appearance thanks to the use of Pilsner malt in the mash and possessed of an enticing herbal, grapefruit and bittersweet character, this is Towcester's best seller and named after the leat that passes beneath the Mill.

#37 XT Brewing

Notley Farm, Long Crendon HP18 9ER
xtbrewing.com | xt@xtbrewing.com | 01844 208310
@XTBrewing @xtbrew @xtbrew

About the brewery

You will find XT Brewing down on the farm, Notley Farm to be precise, hidden away near Oxford with its brewers beavering away to create a wide range of beers.

The 18-barrel brewery opened in 2011, the brainchild of co-owners Gareth Xifaras and Russ Taylor, their surnames the origin of the brewery's name. 'We aim to be an innovative, independent brewery crafting a wide range of beers,' says Taylor, who used to work with Windsor & Eton Brewery. 'Our XT beers form the core range of characterful, full flavoured brews and our wild side – Animal – pushes the boundaries with new and exciting, challenging one-off experimental beers.' Brewing in the countryside obviously makes XT conscious of their stewardship of nature: 'We are as eco-friendly and sustainable as possible,' says Taylor, 'recycling nearly all our waste products and our spent raw materials go to local farmers to feed their cattle and pigs. With reusable casks we also have minimal packaging waste.'

Fancy a day in the country? Then head to XT Brewing, where there is also a shop and comfortable tap room (those sofas look inviting!), where beers such as Hop Kitty or the rich, dark porter Eight can be savoured and then taken home in bottle.

Signature brew

Hop Kitty, 3.9%
Super-hopped pale ale with round after round of Cascade and Citra being added, with the result plenty of tropical fruitiness, a malt sweetness and a dry bittersweet finish with more tropical fruitiness lingering.

Established: 2011
Litres per year: 500,000

Brewery tours: Yes
Taphouse: Yes
Beers produced: 200

Open: Mon - Weds 9.30am - 5pm, Thurs - Sat 9.30am - 6pm

#38 beertorrent®

1 Creative Railway Arches, Court Street, Leamington Spa, Warwickshire CV31 2DH
beertorrent.uk | contact.beertorrent@gmail.com | 01926 930937
@BeerTorrentOfficial @beertorrent @BeerTorrent

About the venue

As well as serving beer in its tap room, beertorrent is a local space and a learning place with meet the brewer events every weekend, a brewing club that meets on the first Tuesday of each month and specialist talks about every aspect of brewing, including the role of oxygen and brewing yeast. What makes beertorrent unique is that it can brew in small batch sizes (45 litres), which means a constantly changing selection of beer styles. Whether you are an aspiring home-brewer or just a curious beer-lover, beertorrent is not to be missed.

Mission statement

Our mission is to spread the craft of artisan brewing. We run brewing courses and provide equipment and ingredients in our shop to make the finest quality beers. We also brew a constantly changing range of specialist beers for our tap room, nestled in a railway arch close to Leamington Spa station. We aim to foster a culture of social brewing in our friendly, all inclusive environment.

Open: Fri 5pm - 9pm,
Sat 5pm - 9pm,
Sun midday - 4pm
Brewing courses by appointment only.

Established: 2015
No. of beers sold: 9 changing taps
Takeout: Yes

Open: Tues - Sat 12 - 7pm
Established: 2018
No. of beers sold: 136
Sit-in: Yes

#39 The Drawing Board Bottle Shop

3 Court Street, Leamington Spa, Warwickshire CV311NH
thedrawingboard.pub | shop@thedrawingboard.pub | 01926 259704
@thedbbottleshop @thedbbottleshop @thedbbottleshop

About the venue

As well as the Drawing Board pub (see overleaf), lucky old Leamington Spa has a bottle shop, which is operated by the same owners. It's a comfortable and slightly quirky place (a Space Invaders machine sits in one corner and there are framed vintage comic books and annuals on the walls) with plenty of great beers from the local likes of Burning Soul, Dig Brew and Purity, as well as Brit craft beer classics such as The Kernel and Siren. Occasional meet the brewer events and tap takeovers add to the fun.

Mission statement

We are the only craft beer focused stockist in Leamington Spa, and we set out to encourage more people to understand and enjoy craft beer. We wanted to find a way of selling more interesting products that we felt were too expensive or niche to sell in The Drawing Board pub itself. We continue to try and sell things that others are not selling, so Japanese whisky is very much our bag!

#40 The Drawing Board

18 Newbold Street, Leamington Spa, Warwickshire CV32 4HN
thedrawingboard.pub | hello@thedrawingboard.pub | 01926 330 636
@thedbleamington @thedbleamington @thedbleamington

About the venue

Award-winning free house and eclectic celebration of independence set over two floors with top end gourmet bar food, a great selection of craft beers (from the likes of Burning Soul, Dig Brew, Old Pie Factory, Purity, Tiny Rebel, DEYA and Brew York) as well as single malts, gins and wines. The decor is part pop art (lots of framed comic book covers) and part stylish but comfortable media club hangout (sofas, armchairs, plants and log-burners), while old annuals from the likes of The Dandy, Top of the Pops and Basil Brush (yes Basil Brush!) line the shelves.

Mission statement

Being an independent free house in Leamington Spa is something really special, we can buy and sell whatever we want from whoever we want. This is a rarity and we relish it. It means offering something individual that others are not. This is what we do. We are not an every pub or a watered down idea of a business, we are the ground floor of an ideal, a chance to show real attention to detail with all that we can. We continue to push the envelope with our beer selection, without forgetting our roots.

Open: Mon - Sat 11am - 11pm, Sun 12 - 10.30pm

Established: 2015
No. of beers sold: 41
Takeout: No

WARMINSTER
INTEGRITY
OF THE
BEER
MALT
WARMINSTER MALTINGS
CHRIS GARRATT, HEAD MALTSTER . TEL: 01985 212014
CHRIS.GARRATT@WARMINSTER-MALT.CO.UK

Warwickshire & Northamptonshire Breweries

Boot Town Brewery c/o Copper Kettle Brewing, Bosworth's Garden Centre, 110 Finedon Road, Burton Latimer, Northamptonshire NN15 5QA
01536 725212 | boottownbrewery.co.uk

Church End Brewery Ridge Ln, Nuneaton, Warwickshire CV10 0RD | 01827 713080
churchendbrewery.co.uk

Church Farm Brewery Church Farm, Church Lane, Budbrooke, Warwickshire CV35 8QL
01926 411569 | churchfarmbrewery.co.uk

Creaton Grange Ales Old Wash House Creaton Grange, Grooms Ln, Creaton, Northampton, Northamptonshire NN6 8NN | 07943 595829
creatongrangeales.co.uk

Digfield Ales Lilford Lodge Farm, Barnwell, Northamptonshire PE8 5SA | 01832 273954
digfield-ales.co.uk

Fosse Way Brewing Company Unit 5a, Manor Farm, Hunningham Road, Offchurch, Warwickshire CV33 9AG
07956 179999 | fossebrew.co.uk

Frog Island Brewery The Maltings, St James' Rd, Northampton, Northamptonshire NN5 5HS
01604 587772 | frogislandbrewery.co.uk

**Great Oakley Brewery Ark Farm, High Street South, Tiffield, Towcester, Northamptonshire NN12 8AB | 01327 351759
greatoakleybrewery.co.uk**

Gun Dog Ales Unit 5b, Great Central Way, Woodford Halse, Northamptonshire NN11 3PZ
01327 264095 | gundogales.co.uk

Hoppy Family Brewery Harcourt Street, Kettering, Northamptonshire NN16 0RS
07986 019579 | hfbrewery.com

King's Cliffe Brewery 10 Kingsmead, King's Cliffe, Peterborough, Northamptonshire PE8 6YH
07843 288088 | kcbale.co.uk

**Maule Brewing Co 4 Derngate, Northampton, Northamptonshire NN1 1UB
01604 637025 | maulebrewing.com**

Nene Valley Brewery 8 Station Rd, Oundle, Peterborough, Northamptonshire PE8 4DE
01832 272776 | nenevalleybrewery.com

Nobby's Brewery 2 Cottingham Way, Thrapston, Kettering, Northamptonshire NN14 4PL
01832 730800 | nobbysbrewery.co.uk

Phipps Northampton Brewery Company
54 Kingswell St, Northampton, Northamptonshire NN1 1PR | 01604 946606
phipps-nbc.co.uk

Potbelly Brewery 31-44 Sydney St, Kettering, Northamptonshire NN16 0HY | 01536 410818 potbelly-brewery.co.uk

Purity Brewing Co Upper Spernall Farm, Spernal Ln, Great Alne, Alcester, Warwickshire B49 6JF | 01789 488007 puritybrewing.com

Purple Cow Brewing 39 Victoria St, Kettering, Northamptonshire NN16 0BU | 07507 398353 purplecowbrewing.co.uk/

Slaughterhouse Brewery (Wild Boar Pub) Bridge St, Warwick, Warwickshire CV34 5PD 01926 490986 | slaughterhousebrewery.com

Three Hills Brewing 4 Thrapston Rd, Woodford, Kettering, Northamptonshire NN14 4HY 07400 706884 | threehillsbrewing.com/

Towcester Mill Brewery Towcester Mill, Chantry Ln, Towcester, Northamptonshire NN12 6YY | 01327 437060 towcestermillbrewery.co.uk

Warwickshire Beer Co Queen St, Cubbington, Leamington Spa, Warwickshire CV32 7NA 01926 450747 | warwickshirebeer.co.uk

Weatheroak Brewery 21a High St, Studley, Warwickshire B80 7HN | 01527 854433 weatheroakbrewery.co.uk

Windmill Hill Brewing Co Radford Semele, Leamington Spa, Warwickshire CV31 1UR 01926 355450 | whbrewery.co.uk

XT Brewing Notley Farm, Long Crendon, Northamptonshire HP18 9ER 01844 208310 | xtbrewing.com

Staffordshire

Key

#41 Burton Bridge Brewery (P116)
#42 Burton Town Brewery (P118)
#43 Heritage Brewing Company (P120)
#44 Lymestone Brewery (P122)
#45 Marston's Brewery (P124)
#46 Slater's Ales (P126)
● Staffordshire breweries (P132)

#41 Burton Bridge Brewery

24 Bridge Street, Burton on Trent, Staffordshire DE14 1SY
burtonbridgebrewery.co.uk | bbb@burtonbridgebrewery.com | 01283 510573
@burtonbridge.brewery

About the brewery

It's hard to escape the past in Burton on Trent: walking towards the brewery and its glorious tap, the Burton Bridge Inn (pg. 130), the brewing heritage of the town is omnipresent. Plaques and signs commemorate long lost breweries and maltings, while the massive conditioning tanks of Molson-Coors (full of Carling) dominate the route.

Like Molson-Coors, Burton Bridge Brewery is very much of the here and now, even if it is one of the oldest survivors of the first micro-brewery boom of the late 1970s and early 1980s, having been set up in 1982 by Geoff Mumford and Bruce Wilkinson, who had both worked in the brewing industry (incidentally it was the 200th brewery to open in Burton since monks started originally making ale at the Abbey centuries before).

'As the years have progressed,' says Mumford, 'our beer range has increased considerably, mainly due to our pioneering production of porters, golden ales and stouts. We can now take beer drinkers on a tasteful journey from golden sunlight through sparkling amber ales into midnight black porter and stouts.'

Take the time to visit the brewery's inn, with its traditional interior, old scenes of Burton breweries on the wall and a sense of community – and most importantly drink Burton Bridge's fine beers and get a sense of their importance to Burton.

Signature brew

Bridge Bitter, 4.2%
This is a classic Burton-style beer with a gentle aroma of malt and fruit giving a good balanced start that finishes with a robust hop mouthful.

Established: 1982
Litres per year: 400,000
Brewery tours: No
Taphouse: Yes
Beers produced: 20
Open: Mon - Thurs 5pm - 11pm, Fri - Sat midday - 11.30pm, Sun midday - 2.30pm, 7pm - 11pm

Established: 2016
Litres per year: 24,000

Brewery tours: Yes
Taphouse: Yes
Beers produced: 10

Open:
Fri midday - 8pm,
Sat midday - 3pm

#42 Burton Town Brewery

8 Falcon Close, Burton on Trent, Staffordshire DE14 1SG
burton.town | hello@burton.town | 01283 510839
@burtontown @burtontownbrewery @BurtonTownBrew

About the brewery

It goes without saying that beer is a major currency in Burton, a rich seam to be tapped, especially helped by its history and the extraordinary water below the town that countless brewing generations have made their own. Burton Town Brewery is one of the latest beneficiaries of this blessed position, a six-barrel microbrewery that has its roots in traditional cask beers, though new releases take inspiration from the best of beers and ingredients around the world.

It also goes without saying that, in the equally best traditions of modern breweries, Burton Town has its own tap room, a roomy modern, elemental-like (bare brick and plenty of wood) space with the brewery at one end. Across one of the walls, with a great awareness of the town's place in the history of beer, there runs a mural depicting the history of brewing in the town. So you can drink deeply of beers such as Modwena and Burton IPA, while learning about how the two turned out the way they did.

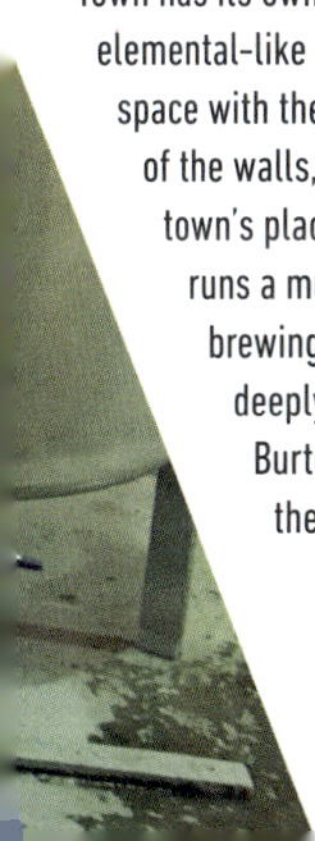

Very educational. And given that Burton Albion FC is a short walk away, if you're on the way to the match why not pop in for a pint of Albion and hope that your side win.

Signature brew

Kölsch, 4.5%
This is a firm all-year-round favourite and a version of the famous Cologne beer. Made to a traditional recipe, it has three German malts and selected noble hops that make it both malty and refreshing.

#43 Heritage Brewing

National Brewery Centre, Horninglow Street, Burton on Trent, Staffordshire DE14 1NG
heritagebrewingcompany.co.uk | sales@heritagebrewingcompany.co.uk | 01283 777006
@Heritage Brewing Company

About the brewery

There still remains a great wealth of brewing information hidden around the UK. Despite the fact that during the great beer defenestrations of the 1960s and 70s, when members of the so-called 'Big Six' (Allied Breweries, Bass Charrington, Courage, Scottish & Newcastle, Whitbread and Watney Mann) bought up family owned regional breweries, closed them down and quite often let their recipes end up in skips, there are still plenty of records available to remind us of what our grandfathers and grandmothers enjoyed on their (frequent) visits to the public house.

This serendipity of surfing the mash tuns and hop backs of time is exactly what gives Heritage Brewing its mission in life. For under the careful eye of veteran master brewer Steve Wellington, brewing history is brought back to life by recreating recipes from the past. To make things even more historical, the brewery is based at the National Brewery Centre in Burton-upon-Trent, where every particle of air you breathe seems to have the soul of beer within. Perhaps a Charrington IPA which Cockneys used to enjoy with a pork pie and a spot of banter, while if you're very lucky you might pick up a re-brew of the classic imperial stout P2. Sometimes, it pays to look backwards while going forwards.

Signature brew

Masterpiece IPA, 5.6%

On the nose, there are aromatic hops, toasted cereal notes and hints of smoke and spice, with the same appearing on the palate enhanced by a fragrant fruity character and a top note of fresh bread. Try it with Stilton.

Established: 2015
Litres per year: 240,000
Brewery tours: Yes
Taphouse: Yes
Beers produced: 8
Open: Brewery: Mon - Fri 8am - 4.30pm, National Brewery Centre Mon - Sun 10am - 5pm (Summer) (- 4pm Winter)

Established: 2008
Litres per year: 219,700

Brewery tours: Yes
Taphouse: Yes
Beers produced: 20

Open: Mon - Fri
7.30am - 4.30pm

#44 Lymestone Brewery

The Old Brewery, Unit 5 Mount Road Industrial Estate, Mount Road, Stone, Staffordshire ST15 8LL
lymestonebrewery.co.uk | mrsbrad@btconnect.com | 01785 817796
@lymestoneales @lymestonebrewery @lymestoneales

About the brewery

Stone is a historic brewing town, which was once home to Bent's Brewery and the original Joule's, both of which closed in the 1970s. However, back in 2009, experienced brewer Ian 'Brad' Bradford and wife Viv rekindled the town's brewing flame when they set up Lymestone and the brewery has since gone from strength to strength.

As well as being a family run business (daughter Sarah also brews and son Harry manages the brewery's brace of pubs), sustainability is high on the agenda for Lymestone, with their mission being 'to produce award-winning quality beers consistently and in a sustainable and environmentally friendly way'. They have a wide range of eco-friendly activities running at both the brewery and their 'community micro pub' the award-winning Borehole, which includes refuse recycling, reusing and reworking of furniture, beer garden development, recycling of crisp packets and plastic-free activities. Oh and there's the beehives on the roof, which has provided honey for Lymestone's chocolate honey beer Stone Brood.

The brewery's other pub, the Lymestone Vaults, is in Newcastle-under-Lyme, a friendly and engaging place where you can drink deeply of Brad's beers as well as those from daughter Sarah's Stray Cat brand. Those who have been on the regular brewery tours and tastings also speak highly of Brad's engaging and positive approach.

Signature brew

Ein Stein, 5%
The brewery's best-seller is a blonde continental style 5% bitter. The combination of pale Maris Otter malt and fresh Hersbrucker hops from Germany creates an ale that will please the palate and quench the thirst.

#45 Marston's Brewery

Shobnall Road, Burton on Trent, Staffordshire DE14 2BG
marstonsbrewery.co.uk | DE14@marstons.co.uk | 01283 531131
@marstonsbrewery @marstonsbrewery @marstonsbrewery

About the brewery

Marston's began making beer in Burton on Trent in 1834, at a time when the town's brewing industry was growing and growing. Part of the attraction was the unique water, which trickled down through a thick layer of gypsum before it was brought back up again through the brewery's own well. This mineral rich water, as other breweries in the town were to discover, gave their beers a depth of flavour, character and crisp refreshing bitterness.

Since then, Marston's has been an integral part of Burton and remains its oldest surviving brewery, a brewing gem where modern mixes happily with the traditional, where oak casks are still used to ferment the flagship Marston's Pedigree whilst a state of the art bottling line packages one in five premium ales drunk in the UK.

While other beers are fermented in closed steel vats, the brewery's flagship ale Pedigree ferments in Union casks, made of prime oak that are specially imported from a single forest in Germany. Each Union cask holds over 150 gallons and is four times bigger than a normal cask. This is part of the Burton Union System, a method of fermentation whereby a series of linked Union casks are positioned beneath a stainless-steel trough. Each Union cask has a 'swan neck' pipe leading from the cask and up and over the trough. Marston's is the last brewery in Burton to maintain this system. Not for nothing is it said: 'No Marston's, no beer. No beer, no Burton.'

Signature brew

Pedigree Amber Ale, 4.5%
First brewed in 1952, when according to the brewery it was initially known as 'P', this is a classic product of Burton on Trent, which is made using the Burton Union System. Delicate caramel on the nose, alongside the famous Burton Snatch, while the palate is biscuity malt, spicy hops and a light fruitiness.

Established: 1834
Litres per year: 70,000,000
Brewery tours: Yes
Taphouse: DE14 - our Visitor Centre
Beers produced: 7 in core range plus seasonal throughout the year
Open: Mon - Sat (see website for full times)

Established: 1995
Litres per year: 380,000
Brewery tours: Yes
Taphouse: Yes
Beers produced: 16
Open: Mon - Fri 8am - 4pm

#46 Slater's Ales

St Albans Road, Stafford, Staffordshire ST16 3DR
slatersales.co.uk | 01785 257 976
@slatersales @slatersales

About the brewery

Ged and Moyra Slater started Slater's back in 1995, when it was originally called the Eccleshall Brewery and based behind the George Hotel in the town of the same name. Business boomed and their beers became popular throughout the Midlands. Growth is always good for beer and so in 2006, the brewery moved to its current home in Stafford and also became better known as Slater's Ales.

The 30-barrel brewery still remains in family hands, though there has been a changing of the guard with Ged's son Andrew now in charge of overseeing beers such as Premium, 1 Hop and Amarillo. During the summer of 2019, the brewery was very excited to install a hop cannon, which as its name might suggest is a bit of brewing kit that enables more hops to be added to Slater's beers. If you want to get a full flavour of the brewery then regular tours can be booked in which tutored tastings of the beers take place close to where they are produced. The brewery also hosts an annual Oktoberfest every October with music, a hog roast and, naturally, plenty of beer with fancy dress encouraged but not compulsory.

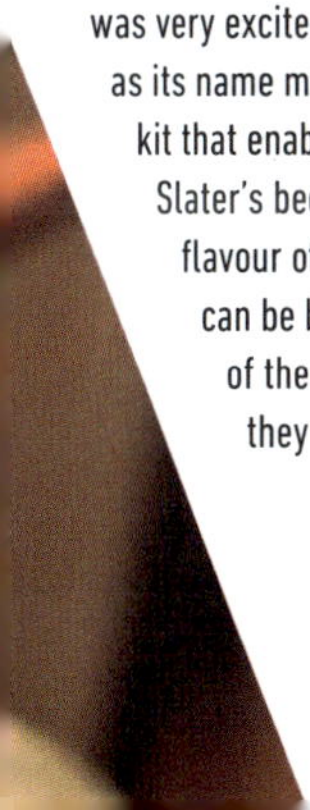

Signature brew

Premium, 4.4%
Brewed continuously since the beginning, this is an amber-hued beer with hints of caramel and fruit on the nose followed by a well-rounded malty mouth feel and bitter finish.

#47 Candid Beer

Units 4 & 5 Woodings Yard, Bailey Street, Stafford, Staffordshire ST17 4BG
candidbeer.co.uk | hello@candidbeer.co.uk | 01785 214289
@candidbeer @candid_beer @candid_beer

About the venue

Candid describes itself as a craft beer bottle-shop and tap room/coffee shop/coworking space/events hub rolled into one. Given that there are six ever-changing draught beer taps and three beer fridges stocked with 100 different canned and bottled beers, all to take out or drink in, Candid offers a complete beer experience. There are also regular beer tastings and meet the brewer events while a coworking monthly membership is available, with the first beer on the house on a Friday evening.

Mission statement

Candid Beer is all about craft beer, community and conversation. At our heart we are a community hub, where people come and meet around our communal table in the tap room to share great beer and great conversations.
Our aim is to never stock the same beer twice, and to help people expand their beer journeys no matter how experienced a craft beer drinker they might be.

Open: Tues - Wed 10am - 7pm, Thurs 10am - 9pm, Fri 10am - 10.30pm, Sat 12.30 - 10.30pm
Established: 2019

No. of beers sold: 100+ cans/bottles in the fridges. Six beers on tap - always changing and never repeated
Sit-in: Yes

Open:
Tues - Sat
10am - 5.30pm,
Sun 10am - 4pm
Established: 2019

No. of beers sold:
10 different types of beers from 23 different breweries.
Sit-in: Yes

#48 The Beer Hut

Grangewood Garden Centre, Bonehill Road, Tamworth, Staffordshire B78 3HP
beerhut1949@gmail.com | 07368 613230
@thebeerhut @thebeerhut @thebeerhut

About the venue

Opening in 2019, The Beer Hut is based in a popular and lively garden centre and sells beers from the likes of Two Towers, Sadler's (including their Peaky Blinder craft lager), Burning Soul and The Backyard Brewery. Occasional beer events are held, such as a recent one that included a tasting of the Peaky Blinder craft lager, which also saw the appearance of a special branded car from the era of the TV series. The Hut also sells various spirits and wines.

Mission statement

We're different because we personally seek locally made and specialist drinks promoting people in a unique establishment. At the moment we've got ten different types of beers from 23 different breweries. We also offer themed events that coincide with the products we sell and work with some businesses to maximise our market base.

#49 The Bridge Inn

24 Bridge Street, Burton on Trent, Staffordshire DE14 1SY
burtonbridgeinn.co.uk | burtonbridgeinn@gmail.com | 01283 536596
@burtonbridgeinn

About the venue

Step into The Bridge Inn and you will be embraced like an old friend by the traditional cosiness of classic pub ambience. There are two rooms, centred around the bar, where the beers of Burton Bridge Brewery take centre stage. The pub was refurbished and expanded in 2002, which won it joint winner in that year's Best Refurbished Pub category run by CAMRA. It has remained a mellow pub, comfortable in its own skin, a proper drinkers' pub with the style of a country pub in town.

Mission statement

To offer great tasting beer in a cosy pub setting - The Bridge Inn was originally a small edge of town centre Bass pub under the sign of the Fox and Goose. To the rear of the pub there were a number of rundown buildings, one of which, a small 1823 dated malthouse, subsequently became our brewhouse. The pub re-opened after the brewery in August 1982 as The Bridge Inn with a Fox and Goose still featuring on the hanging sign.

Open: Mon - Thurs 5pm - 11pm, Fri - Sat midday - 11.30pm, Sun midday - 2.30pm, 7am - 11pm

Established: 1982
No. of beers sold: 8
Takeout: Yes

More on P28-29

Staffordshire Breweries

Blythe Brewery Blythe House Farm, Lichfield Road, Rugeley, Staffordshire WS15 3QQ
07483 248723 | blythebrewery.co.uk

Burton Bridge Brewery **24 Bridge St, Burton on Trent, Staffordshire DE14 1SY | 01283 510573**
burtonbridgebrewery.co.uk

Burton Town Brewery **8 Falcon Cl, Burton on Trent, Staffordshire DE14 1SG**
01283 510839 | burton.town

Freedom Brewery Bagots Pk, Abbots Bromley, Rugeley, Staffordshire WS15 3ER
01283 840721 | freedombrewery.com

Heritage Brewing Company **The National Brewery Centre, Horninglow St, Burton on Trent, Staffordshire DE14 1NG | 01283 777006**
heritagebrewingcompany.co.uk

Lymestone Brewery **The Old Brewery, Mt Industrial Estate, Mount Rd, Stone, Staffordshire ST15 8LL | 01785 813581**
lymestonebrewery.co.uk

Marston's Brewery **Shobnall Rd, Burton on Trent, Staffordshire DE14 2BG | 01902 711811**
marstonsbrewery.co.uk

Morton Brewery Unit 10, Essington Light Industrial Estate, Essington, Staffordshire WV11 2BH | 07988 069647 | mortonbrewery.co.uk

Quartz Brewing Archers, Alrewas Road, Kings Bromley, Staffordshire DE13 7HW
01543 473965 | quartzbrewing.co.uk

Slater's Ales **St Albans Road Industrial Estate, Stafford, Staffordshire ST16 3DR**
01785 257976 | slatersales.co.uk

Staffordshire Brewery Unit 2, Harrison Way, Cheddleton, Leek, Staffordshire ST13 7EF
01538 361919 | staffordshirebrewery.co.uk

Tamworth Brewing Co 29 Market St, Tamworth, Staffordshire B79 7LR | 01827 319872
tamworthbrewing.co.uk

Titanic Brewery Co Unit 5, Callender Pl, Stoke on Trent, Staffordshire ST6 1JL | 01782 823447
titanicbrewery.co.uk

Tower Brewery Glensyl Way, Burton on Trent, Staffordshire DE14 1LX | 01283 562888
towerbrewery.co.uk

Uttoxeter Brewing Co 26B Carter St, Uttoxeter, Staffordshire ST14 8EU | 07734 392321
uttoxeterbrewingcompany.com

Weal Ales 6 Newpark Business Park, London Rd, Chesterton, Newcastle, Staffordshire ST5 7HT
01782 565635 | wealales.co.uk

Wincle Beer Co Tolls Farm Barn, Danebridge, Wincle, Macclesfield, Staffordshire SK11 0QE
01260 227555 | winclebeer.co.uk

The perfect gift for beer lovers
Explore the full range of books
Shop now at thebrewerybible.com
THE BREWERY BIBLE
SOUTH WEST EDITION I

Herefordshire Worcestershire & Shropshire

Key

#50 Bewdley Brewery Ltd (P136)
#51 Joules Brewery (P138)
#52 Ludlow Brewing Co (P140)
#53 The Sociable Beer Company (P142)
#54 Wood's Brewery (P144)
#55 Wye Valley Brewery (P146)
Hereforeshire, Worcestershire & Shropshire breweries (P154)

#50 Bewdley Brewery Ltd

Brewery Craft Centre, Lax Lane, Bewdley, Worcestershire DY12 2DZ
bewdleybrewery.co.uk | sales@bewdleybrewery.co.uk | 01299 405148
@thebewdleybrewerytap @bewdleybrewery

About the brewery

Welcome to Bewdley, a beautiful Georgian town that sits alongside the River Severn as it makes its way southwards to the sea. Let's welcome everyone to Bewdley Brewery as well, a family owned enterprise that is located in an old Victorian school, a brief stroll from the town centre. The brewery opened in 2008, the first in the town since 1912, when the then head brewer William Mucklow produced a 6% mild, which was reputedly the second strongest mild in the country (he is remembered by the current brewery's William Mucklow's Dark Mild, which is also 6%).

As well as the brewery, there is the popular Brewery Tap next door, which always has five beers on hand-pull alongside its in-house lager Laxford, a keg version of Worcestershire Way and cider from Robinson's. This is a place where it pays to spend time studying Bewdley's beers, including the aforementioned William Mucklow's Dark Mild and the 4.5% Sir Keith Park. As you sit in front of your pint, take a look around: the walls of the Tap are decorated with beer, pub and railway memorabilia and you can also see the 10-barrel brewing kit through a viewing glass. And if that's not enough, during the summer months from Easter to September, the brewery hold street food events on every other Saturday. William Mucklow would have been proud of his successors.

Signature brew

Worcestershire Way, 3.6%
Named after the Worcestershire Way 31 mile walk between Bewdley and Malvern, this is a refreshing session ale with citrus overtones.

Established: 2008
Litres per year: 206,000

Brewery tours: Yes
Taphouse: Yes
Beers produced: 12

Open: (Taphouse)
Thurs 4pm - 9pm,
Fri - Sat midday - 9pm
Sun midday - 3pm

#52 Ludlow Brewing Co.

The Railway Shed, Station Drive, Ludlow, Shropshire SY8 2PQ
theludlowbrewingcompany.co.uk | beer@theludlowbrewingcompany.co.uk | 01584 873 291
@ludlow.brewery @ludlowbrewery @ludlowbrewery

About the brewery

Old and new, modernity and heritage come together at the home of Ludlow Brewery. Located in a converted railway shed that was built in 1857, the brewery has been designed by owners Gary and Alison Walters to limit carbon emissions and be as green as possible. All aspects of the brewing process are recycled: heat is reclaimed to heat underfloor heating, solar panels have been installed, while spent grain and hops are sent for animal feed and local gardeners.

The brewery's visitor centre and tap is also in the same building, where the full range of Ludlow's beers can be sampled, in the company of the brewery's gleaming stainless steel equipment, which can produce up to one and a half million pints annually. Such was the effort, innovation and passion that went into the conversion of the railway shed into a brewery and tap, that in 2011 Ludlow Brewery was awarded the Ludlow Heritage Award. With the renovation having been judged to be exemplary in terms of preserving and enhancing the character, through the use of both modern and ancient building materials. It also stated that the high quality craftsmanship upholded the best traditions of construction in the town. Given that Ludlow is perhaps one of the best preserved and architecturally soothing towns in England, this was high praise indeed.

Signature brew

Ludlow Gold, 4.2%
Ludlow's best-selling beer is a rich gold in colour, with tropical fruit on the nose and palate, a creamy mouth feel followed by a bittersweet finish. 'A great easy-drinking session ale that keeps you wanting more!'

Established: 2006
Litres per year: 850,000

Brewery tours: Yes
Taphouse: Yes
Beers produced: 6
Open: Mon - Thurs 10am - 5pm, Fri 10am - 6pm, Sat 10am - 5pm, Sun 11am - 4pm

Established: 2017
Litres per year: 30,000
Brewery tours: On request
Taphouse: Yes
Beers produced: 8
Open: Thurs 5pm - 11pm, Fri 4pm - 11pm, Sat private hire + events - times vary

#53 The Sociable Beer Company

6-8 Britannia Road, Worcester, Worcestershire WR1 3BQ
thesociablebeercompany.com | hello@thesociablebeercompany.com | 07701 355478
@thesociablebeercompany @thesociablebeercompany @SociableBeerCo

About the brewery

Sociable by name, sociable by nature. Founders Jason Clines and Steve Tromans are old friends, who always enjoyed getting together most weekends to drink the home-brew they'd made. After a couple of years, Steve had developed dozens of recipes for different styles of beer, and Jason had lots and lots of friends who liked drinking the beer they had made and one day they decided it was time to take things further!

The Sociable Beer Company was born with a custom-built brewing kit imported from Slovakia and installed in a former police lost property and evidence store in the heart of Worcester. Now, The Sociable Beer Company is the largest brewery and tap room in the city, with 90% of its beer brewed served on the premises, alongside plenty of regular live music nights. 'We aren't trying to be the next Brewdog or Camden Brewery,' says Jason, 'we believe that beer is best served with friends and our ethos is to create a great night out for all our visitors, whether they are celebrating a big birthday, coming to enjoy our weekly music events or just dropping by for a pint and a chat. If you are visiting Worcester, meeting for a Sociable Beer has never been so good!'

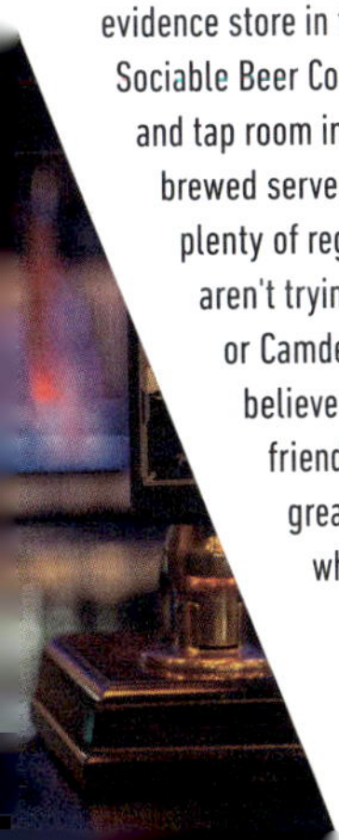

Signature brew

Shindig, 3.6%
Refreshing gold coloured session IPA, which like all the brewery's beers is named after social events (eg, Bash, Wingding, Blow Out).

#54 Wood's Brewery

Wistanstow, Craven Arms, Shropshire SY7 8DG
woodbrewery.co.uk | mail@woodbrewery.co.uk | 01588 672523
@WoodBreweryLtd @thewoodbrewery @WoodsBrewCrew

About the brewery

When Wood's started brewing in 1980, they were one of the early so-called microbreweries at the forefront of a brewing revolution and also went on to become a founding member of SIBA (though it was then called the Small Independent Brewers Association).

The brewery is located (as it was at the start) in outbuildings at the Plough Inn in Wistanstow, which is just outside the small town of Craven Arms. The Plough itself has a history going back to 1774 and was bought by the Wood family in 1968 from the Wrekin Brewery, which ceased brewing a year later; it is here you go to drink beers that have travelled metres from the brewery next door.

Located in the midst of beautiful countryside, Wood's Brewery's beers have always been seen as quintessentially Shropshire, especially with its popular trio of Shropshire Lad, Shropshire Lass and Shropshire Born'n'Bred. It is also responsible for the award winning Ironbridge range of craft beers, which includes Coracle IPA and Kelmis Belgian White. In 2018 Wood's was sold to new owners, who have maintained the brewery's quality and consistency, and made sure that drinkers
in Shropshire and the West Midlands can continue to enjoy beers that have the soul of Shropshire within.

Signature brew

Shropshire Lad, 4.5%
Well-rounded premium bitter with a generous malt character, sweetish overtones followed by a subtle bitterness and fruity notes from the infusion of traditional hops from the neighbouring hop fields of Herefordshire and Worcestershire, First brewed in 1996 to celebrate the centenary of the first publication of A Shropshire Lad by A. E. Housman.

Established: 1980
Litres per year: 400,000
Brewery tours: Yes
Taphouse: Yes
Beers produced: 10
Open: See website for details

Established: 1985
Litres per year: 5,914,706
Brewery tours: Yes
Taphouse: No
Beers produced: 6 core cask, 2 core keg, plus 12 monthly cask specials per year and 6 limited edition keg
Open: Mon - Fri 9am - 5pm

#55 Wye Valley Brewery

Stoke Lacy, Herefordshire HR7 4HG
wyevalleybrewery.co.uk | sales@wyevalleybrewery.co.uk | 01885 490505
@wyevalleybrewery @wyevalleybrewery @wyevalleybrew

About the brewery

It's been 34 years since Wye Valley Brewery was started by former Guinness brewer Peter Amor, when at the start it was ten barrels per week (that's about 2880 pints). Now, an average of 800 barrels a week is being produced, or if you want to talk in pints, about 12 million of them a year.

The brewery's reputation for consistent excellent quality is the reason its beers, including bestsellers HPA and Butty Bach, are served in more than 1200 pubs and bars throughout the West Midlands and South Wales. And, with its range of exciting keg beers becoming increasingly popular in the urban craft bars, the brewery is succeeding in reaching out to both cask and craft beer drinkers!

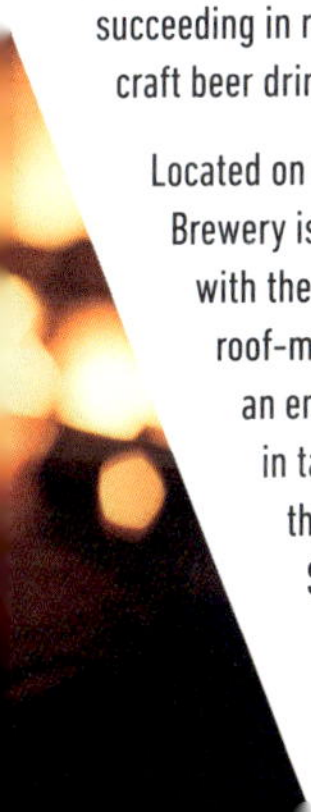

Located on a nine-acre site, Wye Valley Brewery is also about working in harmony with the environment. In addition to roof-mounted solar panels, there is also an entire field of them, both of which in tandem help to generate 57% of the brewery's total energy usage. Spent grain and hops are given to local farmers for animal feed and compost, while excess yeast goes for pig feed. Meanwhile, water vapour created during the brewhouse boil is recovered and used to heat water for cleaning the casks. Take a trip to its visitor centre and taste the beers and you will be at the heart of a great success story.

Signature brew

Butty Bach, 4.5%
Smooth premium ale which is brewed with Maris Otter and Crystal malts, alongside locally grown Fuggles, Goldings and Bramling Cross. Its name is Welsh for 'little friend', so no wonder it's a firm favourite with many of the brewery's friends.

#56 Hop Lord's Taproom & Bottle Shop

7 Pump Street, Worcester, Worcestershire WR1 2QX
hoplord@outlook.com | 07525 445988
@hoplordbottleshop @hoplordbeer @HopLord

About the venue

In 2018 licensee Matt Pugh opened Hop Lord, the first dedicated craft beer shop in Worcestershire. 'We have had over 15 years in the pub trade,' he says, 'and ended up with quite a bit of knowledge and a huge passion for beer.' This enthusiasm means hundreds of excellent beers, tap takeovers and rare beer tastings, including one featuring the highly acclaimed US Tree House Brewing. The shop also has a can seaming machine, enabling customers to take away draught beers in cans.

Mission statement

Our aim is to provide Worcester and the surrounding areas with the beers we like and the best beers we can source. We have a big interest in Bavarian beers, particularly Helles lagers, and stock many. We also have a keen interest in lambic beer and its history. We keep at least 15 in stock in all times and are starting to cellar the rarer ones we find for future tastings later down the line.

Open: Mon - Sun 11am - 9pm
Established: 2018
No. of beers sold: 300
Sit-in: Yes

Open: Sun - Thurs 11am - 11pm, Fri - Sat 11am - 12am

Established: 2010
No. of beers sold: 10
Takeout: Yes

#57 Red Lion Brewery Tap

Great Hales Street, Market Drayton, Shropshire TF9 1JP
bit.ly/JoulesRedLion | brewerytap@joulesbrewery.co.uk | 01630 652602
@joulesredlion @brewerytap2018

About the venue

Come here to explore the full range of Joule's excellent beers and as you sit in the bar you can see through the large windows into the brewery yard and the brew house. A pint or two always sets the appetite on edge and the Red Lion offers great pub food, which is sourced locally and freshly prepared on site. Pork from the Joule's herd at Fordhall Farm is a house speciality, fed on the brewery's spent grains and every Friday complimentary homemade sausage rolls are available on the bar.

Mission statement

Our flagship brewery tap stands proud on Great Hales Street, Market Drayton, and adjoins the brewery. Dating back to 1623, it was an original Joule's house and like most of the medieval town centre, sits over Market Drayton's aquifer, the water source for all our ales. Hard, pure mineral water, found directly beneath the site made the decision where to home the fourth Joule's Brewery very easy.

#58 The Barrels

The Barrels, 69 St Owen's Street, Hereford, Herefordshire HR1 2JQ
wyevalleybrewery.co.uk/our-pubs/the-barrels | info@thebarrels.co.uk | 01885 490505
@thebarrelshereford @thebarrelshereford

About the venue

Once called the Lamb Hotel and owned by West Country Ales, whose enamel plaque is still embedded in the outside wall, The Barrels was renamed in 1985, when Wye Valley Brewery opened at the back. The brewery moved in 2002, and the pub remains a popular hub for beer-lovers with four separate drinking places and a large, partially covered, walled and flag-stoned brewery yard, providing year-round 'alfresco' drinking. The pub also hosts an annual beer festival in aid of local charities and has several darts, pools and skittles teams.

Mission statement

The Barrels is an 18th century coaching inn that is formed partly from the old city wall and is one of the last multi-roomed pubs in Hereford. A down-to-earth drinking establishment, The Barrels was Wye Valley Brewery's home for many years and attracts an eclectic clientele who come for the lively, friendly atmosphere and, of course, excellent beers from Wye Valley Brewery. Landlord Phil Pryce and his team look forward to welcoming you!

Open: Mon - Thur 11am - 11.30pm, Fri - Sat 11am - midnight, Sun midday - 11.30pm

Established: 1986
No. of beers sold: 6
Takeout: No

Open:
Tues - Thur
4 - 11pm,
Fri 4pm - 1am,
Sat midday - 1am,
Sun midday - 11pm

Established: 2016
No. of beers sold: 16 changing taps & 30+ bottles
Takeout: Yes

#59 The Firefly, Hereford

16 King Street, Hereford, Herefordshire HR4 9BX
herefordfirefly@outlook.com | 01432 358252
@firefly.hereford @fireflyhereford @FireflyHereford

About the venue

Even though from the outside it looks like it was once a pub, this was originally a rectory and to compound its spiritual nature it is located a hymn book's throw from the cathedral. However, cast all spiritual thoughts aside as soon as you enter, for this is a place dedicated to the earthly pleasures of good beer and stunning vegan food. Sixteen taps, showcasing various styles of beers, await the thirsty, while regular DJ nights, live music events and tap takeovers add to the hedonistic mix.

Mission statement

We are the Firefly Worcester's little brother in Hereford, serving a range of modern day craft beers and dishing out a vegan street food menu right in the heart of beef country! We pride ourselves on bringing the latest and best breweries to our regular customers and ensuring that the draught beer is served and kept as best as possible and how the breweries intended it to be served.

#60 The Firefly, Worcester

54 Lowesmoor, Worcester, Worcestershire WR1 2SE
fireflyworcester@outlook.com | 01905 616996
@firefly.worcester @Fireflybarworcester @TheFireflyWorc

About the venue

Opening in 2005, the Firefly has become an institution for great beer and food, a place where craft beer fans with massive thirsts make their way to see what the latest releases from the likes of DEYA, Cloudwater and Salopian are (and don't forget ales from the onsite brewery) – think 18 taps of which 14 are on regular rotation showcasing various styles of beers both in cask and keg. Interesting fact: the pub was once home to the night manager for the old vinegar works behind the pub.

Mission statement

We are Worcester's first dedicated craft beer bar, and we also serve a vegan street food menu. We have a year round beer garden and host regular DJ nights, tap takeovers and live music events. We pride ourselves on bringing the latest and best breweries to our regular customers and ensuring that our draught beer is served and kept as best as possible and how the breweries intend it to be served.

Open: Mon - Thurs 3pm - ,midnight, Fri 3pm - 1am, Sat 12pm - 2am, Sun 12 - 11pm

Established: 2005
No. of beers sold: 18 taps & 50 changing bottles
Takeout: Yes

More on P28-29

Herefordshire, Worcestershire & Shropshire Breweries

Ambridge Brewery Priory Piece Piggery, 2A Priory Farm Lane, Priory Farm Lane, Inkberrow, Worcester, Worcestershire WR7 4HT
07500 046391 | ambridgebrewery.co.uk

Bewdley Brewery Ltd **Unit 7, Lax Ln, Bewdley, Worcestershire DY12 2DZ | 01299 405148**
bewdleybrewery.co.uk

Boatlane Brewery 3, Streamside Business Park, Boat Ln, Offenham, Evesham, Worcestershire WR11 8RS | 01386 719558
boatlanebrewery.com

Cannon Royal Brewery Unit 15a, Weston Industrial Estate, Honeybourne, Evesham, Worcestershire WR11 7QB | 01905 621161
cannonroyall.co.uk

Hobsons Brewery Newhouse Farm, Tenbury Road, Cleobury Mortimer, Shropshire DY14 8RD
01299 270837 | hobson-brewery.co.uk

Hop & Stagger Brewery The Old Cow Shed Astol Farm, Norton, Bridgnorth, Shropshire TF11 9EW | 01952 730737
hopandstaggerbrewery.co.uk

Joule's Brewery **(The Red Lion Pub) Great Hales Street, Market Drayton, Shropshire TF9 1JP | 01630 654400**
joulesbrewery.co.uk

Lab Culture Brewery 6 Colemeadow Road, North Moons Moat, Redditch, Worcestershire B98 9PB
01527 362910 | labculture.co.uk

Lakehouse Brewery Peachfield Rd, Malvern, Worcestershire WR14 3LE | 07532 440634
lakehousebrewery.com

Ledbury Real Ales Gazerdine House, Hereford Rd, Ledbury, Herefordshire HR8 2PZ | 01531 671184
ledburyrealales.co.uk

Ludlow Brewing Co **The Railway Shed, Station Drive, Ludlow, Shropshire SY8 2PQ | 01584 873291**
theludlowbrewingcompany.co.uk

Odyssey Brew Co The Brewery, Brockhampton Estate, Worcester, Worcestershire WR6 5SH
01885 483496 | odysseybrewco.com

Pershore Brewery 5 Lyttleton Rd, Pershore, Worcestershire WR10 2DF | 01386 561578
pershorebrewery.com

Salopian Brewing Co Old Station Yard, Old Station Road, Hadnall, Shrewsbury, Shropshire SY4 3DD | 01743 248414
salopianbrewery.co.uk

Six Bells Brewery & Cafe Church St, Bishop's Castle, Shropshire SY9 5AA | 01588 630144
sixbellsbrewery.com

Stonehouse Brewery Weston, Oswestry, Shropshire SY10 9ES | 01691 676457
stonehousebrewery.co.uk

Swan Brewery Enterprise Park, Unit 17, Brunel Rd, Leominster, Herefordshire HR6 0LX
01568 617709 | swanbrewery.co.uk

Teme Valley Brewery Bromyard Rd, Knightwick, Worcester, Worcestershire WR6 5PH
01886 821235 | temevalleybrewery.co.uk

The Friday Beer Co. Link Business Centre, Link Way, Unit 4, Malvern, Worcestershire WR14 1UQ
01684 572648 | thefridaybeer.com

The Hop Shed (Brewery & Tap Room)
The Old Chicken Shed, Suckley, Worcester, Worcestershire WR6 5EQ
01886 884110 | thehopshed.co.uk

The Sociable Beer Company 6 Britannia Rd, Worcester, Worcestershire WR1 3BQ | 07701 355478 | thesociablebeercompany.com

The Three Tuns Brewery Office 8, Enterprise House, Bishops Castle, Shropshire SY9 5AQ
01588 638392 | threetunsbrewery.co.uk

The Wobbly Brewing Co Unit 22C, Beech Business Park, Tillington Road, Hereford, Herefordshire HR4 9QJ | 01432 355318
wobblybrewing.co

**The Wood Brewery Wistanstow, Craven Arms, Shropshire SY7 8DG
01588 672523 | woodbrewery.co.uk**

Woodcote Manor Brewing Co The Brewery at Woodcote Manor, Kidderminster Rd, Dodford, Bromsgrove, Worcestershire B61 9DY
01527 558141 | woodcotemanor.com

Worcester Brewing Company
Arch 49, Cherry Tree Walk, Worcester, Worcestershire WR1 3BH | 07905 221326
facebook.com/Worcesterbrewingcompany

**Wye Valley Brewery Stoke Lacy, Bromyard, Herefordshire HR7 4HG | 01885 490505
wyevalleybrewery,co.uk**

Meet the team

The Brewery Bible's mission is simple - to get more people drinking great local beer.

We are passionate about real food and drink, about provenance, quality and integrity. The Brewery Bible aims to educate and connect you with the world of locally produced beer. Through a series of regional books, our website and our app we hope to do that, and to improve the beer drinking experience for everyone.

Meet the passionate team behind The Brewery Bible, and the Midlands Edition 1.

Nathan Hoare - Co-Founder

With a degree in International Business and experience working with businesses in London, Auckland and Sydney, Nathan returns to Devon to combine his passion for beer and desire to grow a new company. Nathan hopes to work with breweries, beer venues and bottle shops all over the world to enhance the beer drinking experience for business and consumer.

Abby Millar - Co-Founder

Abby's career has been spent helping independent food and drink producers through to national brands tell their unique stories. With experience in artisan spirits and speciality coffee (and a love for hoppy IPAs) Abby will drive The Brewery Bible brand across the globe, helping shape, improve and inspire the beer drinking experience for beer drinkers everywhere.

Greg Hamilton - Co-Founder

After a 10 year career as a senior airline pilot, Greg now focuses on his passion for creating software and delivering exciting user experiences. Whether it's a trendy tap room, fun festival, undiscovered tasting or a simple refreshing pint, Greg is working hard to help people all over the world to connect with, learn about and enjoy memorable beer based experiences through The Brewery Bible app.

Adrian Tierney-Jones

Writes about beer, pubs, food and travel for various magazines and newspapers. He has also written numerous books, including The Seven Moods of Craft Beer and his first ever back in 2002 West Country Ales. Named Beer Writer of the Year 2017, he can be often found standing in front of an audience, glass in hand, telling tales of drinking beer in bars across the world.

Judy Caley

An experienced freelance graphic designer and project manager working across a range of industries undertaking both creative and management tasks for clients worldwide. Specialising within the publishing industry, you'll find Judy looking after projects for a range of clients including well known names such as Penguin, Lonely Planet and Warner Brothers.

Rosie Carmichael

A freelance visual communicator, particularly focused on briefs from within the creative industries including music, events, publishing and editorial. Her work is a combination of digital and analogue processes, resolving into imagery with a playful and nostalgic tone. Visit **rosiecarmichael.com** for more.

Emmy Smith

Emmy is an illustrator from Nottingham, currently living in London. Specialising in digital illustrations around inclusion and positivity (often of women), her work uses fine lines, pastel colours and patterns. Clients include Penguin Random House, Macmillan Publishing and Berlin University.

Be sure to follow us @thebrewerybible for updates on our app, events, future publications and all things beer.

The perfect gift for beer lovers
Explore the full range of books
Shop now at thebrewerybible.com
THE BREWERY BIBLE
SOUTH WEST EDITION I

Tasting Notes

Image credits: all images for listings kindly provided or authorised by owners. Images in editorial pieces supplied by article contributors unless otherwise credited.